DIRTY
JAPANESE

DIRTY JAPANESE

EVERYDAY SLANG FROM "WHAT'S UP?" TO "F*%# OFF!"

•••••Matt Fargo

Illustrated by Lindsay Mack

Ulysses Press

Published by:
Ulysses Press
P.O. Box 3440
Berkeley, CA 94703
www.ulyssespress.com

ISBN10: 1-56975-565-5
ISBN13: 978-1-56975-565-5
Library of Congress Control Number: 2006903813

Printed in Canada by Webcom

10 9 8 7 6 5 4 3

Acquisitions Editor: Nick Denton-Brown
Managing Editor: Claire Chun
Japanese Editor: Seigo Nakao
Editor: Richard Harris
Proofreader: Mark Rhynsburger
Editorial Associates: Elyce Petker, Laurel Shane
Interior Design and Layout: what!design @ whatweb.com
Cover Design: Double R Design
Front Cover Photography: ©clipart.com
Back Cover Illustration: Lindsay Mack

Distributed by Publishers Group West

タンズマン博士に捧げます

Soli Tansman Gloria

TABLE OF CONTENTS

·····Acknowlegments

I'd like to thank Professor Alan Tansman for being as generous as he is wise, Charlie Emrich, Matthew Suidan, Tami Downes and Brooke Ray Smith for putting up with ridiculous questions about human anatomy, Alice for teaching me to love again, Nakayama Risa for advice about anime and manga, Seigo Nakao for his sagacious vetting, Oooka Hironori for being absurdly handsome, Ito Gabin for blowing my mind, Zach Anderson and Aaron Cavin for their cylindrical beards, all the people at Ulysses Press for tolerating my dirty mouth, and of course Kameko for her ineffable shell. I love you all.

USING THIS BOOK

I wrote this book assuming that you already know at least enough Japanese to get by. Maybe you've spent enough time in Japan to get the hang of the basics. Or maybe you nerded out on so much anime that you acquired the entire Gundam vocabulary through osmosis. Or listened to those "Learn Japanese in 24 Hours" CDs until you can order blowfish sashimi without batting an eyelid. Whatever, this book is designed to expand your Japanese past the edge of conventional learning methods.

One thing about the Japanese language, which you'll find me repeating all through this book—it's very, very contextual. What you say depends on who you are speaking to, and this book is meant to be used in the company of friends. So be warned that if you say any of the words and phrases in *Dirty Japanese* to someone older than you, or to a stranger of any age, you can expect them to look at you as if you'd just peed in their kitchen sink.

But when you're among friends or fellow debauchers, let's face it—"*Konnichiwa, yoroshiku onegai shimasu*" is going to make you stand out like... well... a foreigner.

So *Dirty Japanese* is all about the up-to-date slangish words, super-casual phrases, sexy sayings, and innuendos that you aren't going to find anywhere else. (And yes, there's some just plain rude, deficky stuff too. Fuck it—readers with delicate sensibilities can skip over those pages and still get plenty of benefit from the rest of the book.)

Each word or phrase in English is followed by its Japanese equivalent, first as it's written in Japanese characters and then spelled out in the Roman alphabet. A lot of people

((((READING JAPANESE))))

If you haven't tackled the challenge of learning to read Japanese yet, it's not as hard as it looks like it should be. Japanese writing uses three (or maybe four) different sets of characters.

HIRAGANA, full of loops and curves, is an "alphabet" made up of 46 characters representing every sound in the Japanese language—a, i, u, e, o, ka, ki, ku, ke, ko, sa, shi, su, se, so, ta, chi, tsu . . . and so on. It is usually used for writing basic Japanese words. The following words are written in hiragana:

おっす	ossu	What's up!
あんぽんたん	ampontan	dorkface
いそぎんちゃく	isoginchaku	sea anemone

KATAKANA, a simple, angular "alphabet," also has 46 characters. Each one corresponds to a hiragana character, though there can be subtle differences in pronunciation that you don't really need to worry about. It is usually used for writing borrowed foreign words (like "computer"), foreign names, company names, and newly coined Japanese words (like "karaoke"). Here are some examples of katakana:

バイアグラ	baiagura	Viagra
トム・クルーズ	tomu kurūzu	Tom Cruise
ラーメン	rāmen	ramen

who speak pretty decent Japanese can't read a word of it—and you don't really need to. Well, not unless you hope to find your way around Tokyo on your own. You can still get everything in this book from the Roman alphabet versions.

Now take your *Dirty Japanese* and get dirty with it!

KANJI, which looks very complicated, is a set of "ideograms" imported from China as early as the 5th century. There are thousands of kanji characters, and many of them can be pronounced in different ways, depending on context. Good luck. Fortunately, teachers say you only need to know 1945 kanji characters for complete Japanese literacy. Most of the others are only used to represent the names of specific places and people, so you can think of them as corporate logos and only learn to recognize the ones you need. For example:

女子高生	joshi kōsei	schoolgirl
美人薄命	bijin hakumei	beautiful women have unfortunate fates
喧嘩上等	kenka jōtō	tough motherfucker

ROMANJI, the Roman (English) alphabet, is now spreading to Japan because of globalization. You'll encounter it in Japanese slang, especially for writing abbreviations and acronyms of American words and high-tech terms.

You'll find complete lists of hiragana and katakana characters, along with the basic kanji characters, in the front or back of most standard Japanese–English phrasebooks. Study them and challenge yourself to relate them to the words and phrases in this book. I hereby promise that anybody—even Americans—can learn to read hiragana and katakana in about a week, if sufficiently inspired.

(((((PRONOUNCiNG JAPANESE)))))

Japanese grammar may be mind-boggling, but at least the words are easy to pronounce. Once your tongue gets used to the basic syllables, you should be able to read out loud from this or any other phrasebook well enough so local people can understand you.

Japanese has the same five vowels as English, and almost all words end with a vowel or an "n." Each vowel has only one pronunciation:

a = short "a" as in "vagina"

i = "ee" as in "amigo"

u = "oo" as in "lunatic"

e = short "e" as in "ex-girlfriend"

o = regular "o" as in "Oh baby, oh baby, oh baby!"

Sometimes, when reading Japanese words written in the Roman alphabet, you'll see a vowel with a straight line (a macron) above it, like "ā" or "ō." This doesn't change the pronunciation or emphasis, it only means the vowel is drawn out longer. So "ō" means "Ohhh . . . ," not "Oooo . . . ." In addition, the spaces between romanized Japanese words are totally arbitrary. Try to let the syllables flow at a relatively even pace.

Consonant sounds in Japanese are pretty much the same as in English, and there are fewer of them (though many Japanese characters represent combinations of consonants). The consonants that Americans tend to have trouble with are:

ts = like an "s" beginning with a little tongue click, less pronounced than "itsy-bitsy" in English.

n = drawn out longer than an English "n," like "Nnno . . . I don't think so."

r = with the pretense of a roll, as in Spanish.
(This is the letter Americans find hardest to say correctly.)

But if you blow your pronunciation of these letters, people will still be able to understand you. They'll just make fun of your American accent behind your back.

The most important point to remember is that every syllable in Japanese words gets equal emphasis. It's "ka-wa-sa-ki," not "KA-wa-SA-ki."

CHAPTER 1

HOWDY JAPANESE

CHIWASSU NIHONGO
ちわっす日本語

•••••Hello
konnichiwa
こんにちは

Japanese slang isn't really used with strangers, so there aren't a lot of meet-and-greet-type slang words. If you're being introduced to somebody for the very first time, you gotta suck it up and settle for a good old-fashioned *konnichiwa*. But when you're rolling with friends, "hello" will come off a little stiff, so try slinging one of the following slang variations on *konnichiwa*:

Hi
koncha
こんちゃ

Howdy
chiwassu
ちわっす

Howdy-ho
konchassu
こんちゃっす

Howdy-do
nchatt
んちゃっ

·····What's up?
ossu
おっす

A slangier way of saying "hello" would be *ossu*. Like its English counterpart "what's up," *ossu* has an infinite number of variations. *Ossu* was originally an incredibly formal word, the kind of thing that a soldier would say to a drill sergeant— like: "SIR YES SIR!" But in a slang context, *ossu* comes across as a silly way to say "hi." Here's how two friends might greet each other, for example:

Whattup! (greeting)
ossu
おっす！

'Sup. (response)
ussu
うっす。

or

Whazzap! (greeting)
uissū
ういっすー！

Whazzaaaaaaap!!! (response)
ussussu
うっすっす！

····· Good morning / Good evening
ohayō / kombanwa
おはよう・こんばんは

There are also informal variations on "good morning" and "good evening":

Good morning, Sunshine!
ohhā
おっはー

G'morning!
ohayōn
おはよーん

Evenin'
konbancha
こんばんちゃ

····· Long time no see
ohisashiburi
おひさしぶり

As in English, the next part of a greeting usually involves inquiring about the other person's well-being.

Long time no see!
ohisa
おひさ！

How's it hanging?
chōshi dōyo?
調子どうよ？

It's hanging.
bochibochi denna
ぼちぼちでんな。

How you been?
ogenko?
おげんこ？

Same as always, man.
ai kawarazu dayo
相変わらずだよ。

And just as fat as always.
ai kawarazu debu dashi
相変わらずデブだし。

And you're just as retarded as always.
omae wa ai kawarazu aho dashi
お前は変わらずアホだし。

Yo, guys!
yō omaera
よーお前ら！

Hey.
yā
やー！

It's been a while.
hisa bisa dana
久々だな。

What's the word?
saikin dōyo?
最近どうよ？

Same old bullshit.
dōmokōmo nēyo
どうもこうもねーよ。

秋 危
犬 花

·····Goodbye
sayōnara
さようなら

When it comes to parting phrases, there are also any number of variations on the traditional *sayōnara*.

Buh-bye
bainara
ばいなら

See ya
hon jā ne
ほんじゃーね

Later
mata nē
またねー

Smell you later (tough guy way of saying "bye")
aba yo
あばよ

·····Hey!
oi!
おい！

In British English, "oi" is a slightly impolite word used to get people's attention. In Japanese, *oi* is a slightly impolite word used to get people's attention. Go figure. Other attention grabbers:

Look!
hora
ほら！

Hey, kid...
na kimi
な、君。

Come here a sec.
chotto oide
ちょっとおいで。

I want to have a word with you.
hanashi ga arundakedo
話があるんだけど。

·····Myself
jibun
自分

One of the great things about Japanese is the variety of personal pronouns you can assume. The main three ways to say "I" are:

I (feminine/polite)
watashi
私

I'm Nancy!
watashi wa nanshī dēsu
私はナンシーでーす。

I (boyish)
boku
僕

I'm studying as hard as I can to get into college!
boku wa isshō kemmei juken benkyō o yatte māsu
俺は一生けんめい受験勉強をやってまーす 。

I (manly)
ore
俺

I totally look like Mel Gibson, don't I?
ore tte meru gibuson ni nitenē
俺って、メルギブソンに似てねえ？

Of course, there are also numerous slang ways to say "I," most of which are variations on the aforementioned pronouns. Kids use all of these with different levels of irony, but *nobody* just sticks to one pronoun. Especially girls—they can use male pronouns without any innuendo, though a dude's use of a female pronoun will probably be construed as super gay.

I (male, redncck)
ora
おら

I don't know how to use them microwaves.
ora denshi renji no tsukaikata nanka wakannē
おら、電子レンジの使い方なんかわかんねー。

I (male, dopey)
oira
おいら

I went to New York, but I didn't see no big apples.
oira nyūyōku ni ittakedo ōkina ringo nanka minakatta ze
おいら、NYに行ったけど、大きなリンゴなんか見なかったぜ。

I (female, slightly Valley Girl)
atashi
あたし

Oh my god, I have no idea what I did all day!
uwa **atashi** kyō ichinichi nani yatteita ka wakannai no
うわ、あたし、今日一日何やっていたかわかんないの！

I (female, rich girl)
atai
あたい

I always take taxis because I can't stand trains.
atai densha wa iya dakara itsumo takushī o tsukatte iru noyo
あたい、電車は嫌だからいつもタクシーを使っているのよ。

I (male, geezer)
asshi
あっし

You know, I used to be quite the ladies' man, back in the day.
asshi wa mukashi kanari no iro otoko datta ze
あっしは昔、かなりの色男だったぜ。

·····Sorry
gomen nasai
ごめんなさい

Apologizing is a really just a matter of sincerity. If you truly regret your actions, just say so in a straightforward and honest manner. But if you just don't give a fuck, try apologizing with one of the following variations on *gomennasai*:

Sorry, Charlie
gomenchai
ごめんちゃい

Ex-squeeze me
gomenkusai
ごめんくさい

Whoopsy-daisy
mengo mengo
めんごめんご

·····Excuse me
sumimasen
すみません

"Excuse me" is one of those multipurpose words that can be a greeting, a good-bye, or an apology for farting. The same goes for Japanese—you can use these slang variations of "excuse me" in a variety of situations.

Pardon
suimasen
すいません

Well pardon me for living!
ikitete suimasen
生きててすいません！

'Scuse me
suman
すまん

'Scuse my shitty Japanese.
nihongo ga hetakuso de suman
日本語がへたくそですまん。

$0rr¥ *
sumaso
スマソ

$0rr¥ I'm late.
osoku natte **sumaso**
遅くなってスマソ。
*computer speak that went mainstream

Aside from "sorry" and "excuse me," there are a couple other slangish ways to shrug off guilt:

pay no mind
donmai
ドンマイ

My bad
warīne
わりぃーね

Apologies
mōshiwake
もうしわけ

You poor thing
kawaisō
かわいそう

·····Please
kudasai
…ください

Asking for a favor is another of those things that you usually want to be polite about. But when you are talking to friends, feel free to be a little more casual:

Why don't you. . .
. . . kuri
…くり

Why don't you call me sometime.
. . . kondo denwa shite **kuri**
今度電話してくり。

Purdy-please (archaic, rural)
. . . kunro
…くんろ

Tell me your name, **purdy-please!**
onamae osēte **kunro**
お名前おせーてくんろ！

Pretty-please (feminine)
. . . cho
…ちょ

When you find out where the party is, could you text me, **pretty-please?**
nomikai no basho kimattara mēru shite **cho**
飲み会の場所決まったらメールしてちょ。

Do
. . . na
…な

Go **do** your best—we're all rooting for you.
ōen shiterukara gambatte ki**na**
応援してるから、がんばってきな。

Do clean up—I've got friends coming over.
tomodachi ga kuru kara sōji shi**na**
友達が来るから、掃除しな。

I hope you...
...kureya
…くれや

I hope you hang out with me a lot.
takusan asonde **kureya**
たくさん遊んでくれや。

You should. . .
...okure
…おくれ

You should come kick it at my place sometime.
kondo uchi e asobi ni kite **okure**
今度うちへ遊びに来ておくれ。

Snease (a horrible pun)
...chommage
…ちょんまげ

Forgive me, **snease**!
yurushite **chommage**
許してちょんまげ。

Pleeze (slightly silly)
...kurahai
…くらはい

Pleeze eat the leftover sushi.
osushi nokotta kara kutte **kurahai**
お寿司残ったから食ってくらはい。

((((((INTRODUCING YOURSELF))))))
自己紹介 JIKO SHŌKAI

My name's Kenneth.
ore wa kenesu tte iunda
俺はケネスっていうんだ

I'm from Canada.
kanada kara kiteru
カナダから来てる

I only have three months to live.
inochi wa ato sankagetsu shika nainda
命は後３ヶ月しかないんだ。

And I'm still a virgin.
mada cherī dashi
まだチェリーだし。

+++++

My name's Rebecca.
atashi wa rebekka desu
あたしはレベッカです。

I'm from England.
igirisu jin desu
イギリス人です。

I'm here looking for adventure.
bōken o motome koko ni yatte kita
冒険を求めここにやってきた。

No man can handle me.
atashi o atsukaeru otoko nanka inai
あたしを扱える男なんかいない。

·····Let's be friends

yoroshiku onegai shimasu
よろしくお願いします

Okay, so literally this phrase doesn't mean "let's be friends," but that's the best English equivalent I can offer. (A literal translation would go something like "I hope you will take care of things in a manner that is convenient for both of us.") When I learned Japanese as a kid, my teacher gave it the almost as unwieldy rendering. "Please be kind to our friendship." Basically, it's a word that appeals to someone's generosity. You use it after introducing yourself to someone for the first time, or when you ask a favor of somebody who's already your friend. When you say *yoroshiku* to a friend, it just means something like "do me right, baby," as in the following:

> My name's Francisco.
> **Please take care of me** while I'm here in Japan.
> boku wa furanshisuko desu. nihon ni iru aida wa **yoroshiku** desu
> 僕はフランシスコです。 日本にいる間は
> よろしくです。

> I don't know much Japanese,
> so **work with me as best you can.**
> nihongo wa amari wakaranai node **yoroshiku**
> 日本語はあまりわからないのでよろしく。

In other words, *yoroshiku* is an all-purpose phrase that you can use whenever you need to implore somebody's altruism. There are also numerous slang versions of the word:

> **Take good care** of my luggage, now.
> nimotsu **yoroshiko**
> 荷物よろしこ！

> **That would be awesome** if you could hook me up with a cute guy!
> kondo kawaī otoko no ko shōkai shite. **shikoyoro**
> 今度かわいい男の子紹介して。 しくよろ！

I'm gonna drop by tomorrow, so... **(don't ass out on me)**
ashita wa asobi ni iku node **yoropiko**
明日は遊びに行くのでよろぴこ。

·····Nice to meet you
hajimemashite
はじめまして

Not to sound like a broken record, but in Japan *you don't
use slang with someone you don't know.* Which means
that when you are asking somebody how old they are,
where they grew up, or whether they prefer Diet or regular
Dr. Pepper, you probably need to use polite speech. Here
are some basic non-slang icebreakers to use with new
acquaintances.

Nice to meet you.
hajimemashite
はじめまして。

What's your **name?**
onamae nante iundesuka
お名前何ていうんですか？

Have we **met** before?
dokka de **atta** koto arimasenka
どっかで会ったことありませんか？

Do you have a **light?**
raitā arimasuka
ライターありますか？

Do you have the **time?**
jikan wakarimasuka
時間わかりますか？

Thanks. I just wanted to record the exact time I first met you.
arigatō. anata ni hajimete atta jikan o seikaku ni kiroku shite
okikattandesu
ありがとう。あなたに初めて会った時間を正確
に記録しておきたかったんです。

Do you **come here** often?
yoku **kokoni kuru**ndesuka
よくここに来るんですか？

Do you want to get **a drink?**
ocha shimasenka
お茶しませんか？

How old are you?
oikutsu desuka
おいくつですか？

No waaaay! You don't look a day older than twenty!
ussō. hatachi nimo mieani noni
うっそぉ…！２０歳にも見えないのに！

How old do you think **I look?**
watashi wa ikutsu ni **miemasuka**
私はいくつに見えますか？

I'm new to **Japan.**
watashi wa **nihon** ni kita bakkari nandesu
私は日本に来たばっかりなんです。

I **want to make** some Japanese friends.
nihonjin no tomodachi o **tsukuritain** desu
日本人の友だちを作りたいんです。

What do you like to do on your **days off?**
kyūjitsu wa itsumo nani shite imasuka
休日はいつも何していますか？

Teach me some fun **words.**
nanika omoshiroi **kotoba** o oshiete kudasai
何か、おもしろい言葉を教えてください。

I'm **enjoying** hanging out with you.
issho ni asondete **tanoshī** desu
一緒に遊んでて楽しいです。

····· Pictures
shashin
写真

Let's take a picture.
issho ni **shashin** torō
一緒に写真撮ろう。

You know Japanese folks love their pictures. But when you take a photo, don't ask your models to say "cheese"—ask them what one plus one is, because the Japanese word for "two" (*ni*) pulls the old cheeks up like a good face-lift:

What's one plus one?
ichi tasu ichi wa
1 たす 1 は？

Two!
nī
にぃ… !

CHAPTER 2

FRIENDLY JAPANESE

NAKA YOSHI NIHONGO

仲良し日本語

·····Friends
nakama
仲間

Japan is often seen as a rigid society, where social pressures deny people their full range of expression. This is not true. What is acceptable to say depends on who's around. When you're with friends, you can say some of the stupidest shit possible and be loved and forgiven. But even with friends there are different levels of intimacy, as in the following:

Total stranger
aka no tanin
赤の他人

Hey—Japanese folks don't just go up and talk to **total strangers** like that.
anone nihonjin wa sōyatte **aka no tanin** ni koe o kaketari shinai no
あのね、日本人はそうやって赤の他人に声をかけたりしないの。

Acquaintance
shiriai
知り合い

I first got interested in Japan because I had lots of Japanese **acquaintances.**
nihon ni kyōmi o motta no wa nihonjin no **shiriai** ga ōkatta kara da
日本に興味を持ったのは、日本人の知り合いが多かったからだ。

Classmate
dōkyūsei
同級生

Do you hang out with your **classmates** much?
dōkyūsei to wa yoku asondeiru no
同級生とはよく遊んでいるの？

Coworker
dōryō
同僚

Do you get along with your **coworkers?**
dōryō to wa naka yoku shiteru
同僚とは仲良くしてる？

Have you ever dated a **coworker?**
dōryō to tsukiatta koto aru
同僚と付き合ったことある？

Buddy-buddy
naka yoshi
仲良し

You know, we really **get along well.**
uchira tte kekkō **nakayoshi** da ne
うちらってけっこう**仲良し**だね。

Solid guy
ī yatsu
いいヤツ

He's really a **solid guy.**
aitsu wa hontō ni **ī yatsu** da
あいつは本当に**いいヤツ**だ。

Sweet girl
ī ko
いい子

She's really a **sweet girl.**
kanojo wa hontō ni **ī ko** de ne
彼女は本当に**いい子**でね。

Friend
tomodachi
友だち

Seriously, man, you are such a good **friend.**
omae wa hontō ni ī **tomodachi** da
お前は本当にいい**友だち**だ。

Text friend (literally: "thumb-buddy")
oyatomo
オヤトモ

I've got more **text friends** than real friends.
jissai no tomodachi yori **oyatomo** no hō ga ōi
実際の友だちより**オヤトモ**の方が多い。

Text friend (another word for...)
merutomo
メルトモ

Best friend
shin'yū
親友

My **best friend** is Japanese.
shin'yū wa nihonjin da
親友は日本人だ。

((((((((((LiP SERViCE))))))))))
OSEJI お世辞

Meeting new people is fun, but let's be honest: you don't want to know about their master's thesis and they don't want to know about your bottle cap collection. So let's do our best to keep conversation to insincere compliments with the following phrases:

That's a cute skirt you're wearing.
sono sukāto kawaī ne.
そのスカート、かわいいね。

You look kind of like a Japanese Brad Pitt.
anata wa burapi no nihonjin ban da
あなたはブラピの日本人版だ。

You would be super popular in America.
amerika ja zettai moteru yo ne
アメリカじゃ絶対モテるね。

Damn girl, you've got some great fashion sense!
mecha oshare da, kimi
めちゃお洒落だ、君！

I just know I've seen your face in the movies before.
zettai ni eiga de mita koto aru wa, kono kao
絶対に映画で見たことあるわ、この顔。

I never really understood the appeal of Japanese men until I saw you.
nihon no otoko no hito no miryoku ga wakaranakatta, anata ni au made wa
日本の男の人の魅力がわからなかった、あなたに
会うまでは。

Tight bros/girls from way back
osana najimi
幼なじみ

We are **tight from way back.**
koitsu to wa **osana najimi** da
こいつとは**幼なじみ**だ。

Crush
sukina hito
好きな人

I think he's got a new **crush.**
aitsu wa **sukina hito** ga dekita mitai
あいつは**好きな人**ができたみたい。

Boyfriend
kareshi
彼氏

Your **boyfriend** seems like a really nice guy.
kimi no **kareshi** wa yasashisō dane
君の**彼氏**は優しそうだね。

Man (boyfriend)
danna
ダンナ

My **man** doesn't like meeting my friends.
danna ga atashi no tomodachi ni aitagaranainda
ダンナがあたしの友だちに会いたがらないんだ。

Girlfriend
kanojo
彼女

I had a feeling your **girlfriend** was gonna be hot.
omae no **kanojo** tte yappari bijin dane
お前の**彼女**って、やっぱり美人だね。

My girl
yome
ヨメ

I'll introduce you to **my girl** sometime,
but she's not much to look at.
yome wa kondo shōkai surukedo amari kawaiku naindayo
ヨメは今度紹介するけど、あまりかわいくない
んだよ。

Fuck buddy
sefure
セフレ

You know, a **fuck buddy** is the greatest thing a person can
have.
yo no naka de mottomo arigatai sonzai wa yappari **sefure**
dana
世の中で最もありがたい存在はやっぱりセフレ
だな。

•••••Titles
keishō
敬称

Thanks to *Karate Kid*, everybody knows that adding "san" to
Daniel's name makes him "Mister Daniel." But did you know
that there are a bunch of other titles you can add to people's
names—and not just respectful ones either, but slang ones
to use with your friends?

SENSEI ⋯先生
Generally used for teachers, or someone who has
otherwise been a beacon of knowledge in one's life.

SAN ⋯さん
Pretty much the equivalent of "Mister," it maintains
professional distance.

SAMA … さま
"Sir/Madam." Only for highly polite situations, or when you're being ironic.

KUN … くん
An affectionate ending for a friend's name, usually a male friend who is the same age or younger than you.

CHAN … ちゃん
More affectionate and cuter that "kun," and therefore often used with girls, but with boys as well, when they are being cute.

CHIN … ちん
This is a slangier version of "chan."

TAN … たん
And even slangier version of "chan."

PON … ぽん
A silly ending for a friend's name, kind of dorky and fun.

▪▪▪▪▪ Family
kazoku
家族

Family is what it's all about—especially in Japan, where the family unit still retains a subtle semblance of cohesiveness. When speaking about or to your own family, it's normal to use slang titles like "my old lady" or "the geezer"—but be sure to use respectful names like "father" and "mother" when speaking about other people's families.

Father
otōsan
お父さん

What does your **father** do for a living?
otōsan wa donna shigoto shite irundesuka
お父さんはどんな仕事しているんですか。

Dad
papa
パパ

My **dad**'s been married three times.
papa wa sankai mo kekkon shite iru
パパは三回も再婚している。

Old man, geezer
oyaji
親父

My **old man** was a lush.
uchi no **oyaji** wa aruchū datta
うちの親父はアル中だった。

oyaji gyagu
親父ギャグ

a "geezer pun." In Japan, bad puns are referred to as
"geezer puns," as the chief culprits are usually old men.

Mother
okāsan
お母さん

Do you look more like your father or your **mother?**
otōsan to **okāsan** no dotchi ni nite irundesuka
お父さんとお母さんのどっちに似ているんです
か？

Mom
mama
ママ

I miss my **mom**'s cooking.
uchi no **mama** no teryōri ga natsukashikute
うちのママの手料理が懐かしくて。

Old lady
ofukuro
おふくろ

My **old lady** used to be pretty hot, back in the day.
ore no **ofukuro** nanka wakai koro wa chō bijin datta
俺のおふくろなんか、若い頃は超美人だった。

Japanese folks don't do the whole "Yo momma" shtick, but I've seen elementary kids throw out the following zinger in fits of passion:

Your momma's bellybutton is an outie!
omae no kāchan debeso daa
お前の母ちゃん デベソだぁ！

····· Characters
kyara
キャラ

Personally, I like to judge people by how much money they have. But there are actually several other ways to classify our fellow human beings, including the color of their skin and how tall they are. Here are some different ways to describe people:

Spoiled brat
obotchama
おぼっちゃま

That dude is a **spoiled brat.**
aitsu wa **obotchama** dakara na
あいつは**おぼっちゃま**だからな。

Daddy's little princess
ojō
お嬢

That girl is **Daddy's little princess.**
anoko wa **ojō** dakara na
あの子は**お嬢**だからな。

Rich
kanemochi
金持ち

You must be **rich!**
anta **kanemochi** daro
あんた、**金持ち**だろ！

Poor
bimbō
貧乏

It's impossible to be **poor** and live in Tokyo.
tōkyō wa **bimbō** na ningen ja yatte ikenai
東京は**貧乏**な人間じゃやっていけない。

Gaudy
hade
派手

Americans like **gaudy** stuff.
amerikajin wa **hade** na mono ga suki dane
アメリカ人は**派手**なものが好きだね。

Plain
jimi
地味

I like to dress really **plain.**
ikanimo **jimi** na yōfuku ga suki da
いかにも**地味**な洋服が好きだ。

Genius
tensai
天才

You're a goddamn **genius!**
omae wa **tensai** da
お前は**天才**だ。

Airhead
ten'nen
天然

You are such an **airhead.**
omae wa maji de **ten'nen** da
お前はマジで**天然**だ。

The word ten'nen (天然) really just means "natural," but it's often used as an abbreviation for ten'nen boke (天然ボケ) or "natural-born idiot."

Jock
supōtsuman
スポーツマン

I was a total **jock** in high school.
kōkō jidai wa chō **supōtsuman** dattanda
高校時代は超**スポーツマン**だったんだ。

Prettyboy
ikemen
イケメン

She hangs out with lots of **prettyboys.**
kanojo no tomodachi ni wa **ikemen** ga ōi
彼女の友だちには**イケメン**が多い。

Nerd
otaku
オタク

Now I'm just a regular old **nerd.**
ima wa goku ippantekina **otaku** nanda
今はごく一般的な**オタク**なんだ。

Friendly
hito atari ī
人当たりいい

She's a really **friendly** gal.
anoko **hito atari ī** yone
あの子、**人当たりいい**よね。

Antisocial
tsukiai warui
付き合い悪い

He's kind of **antisocial.**
aitsu wa chotto **tsukiai warui** yo
あいつはちょっと**付き合い悪い**よ。

Party animal
asobinin
遊び人

All of my friends are **party animals.**
tomodachi wa minna **asobi'nin** nanda
友だちはみんな**遊び人**なんだ。

Slacker
pūtarō
プー太郎

I graduated three years ago but I'm still a jobless **slacker.**
sannen mae ni sotsugyō shitakedo mada **pūtarō** shiteru
３年前に卒業したけどまだ**プー太郎**してる。

Loser
dame ningen
ダメ人間

What are you doing with a **loser** like him?
aitsu no yōna **dame ningen** to tsukiatte dō sunno
あいつのような**ダメ人間**とつきあってどうすんの？

Responsible adult
shakaijin
社会人

All my friends have turned into **responsible** adults.
tomodachi wa minna **shakaijin** ni natchimatta yo
友だちはみんな**社会人**になっちまったよ。

The word *shakaijin* (**社会人**) means a full-fledged member of society—in other words, someone with a full-time job.

Compare this to jobless slackers known as *pūtarō* (プー太郎).

Businessman
rīman
リーマン

My dad is just a regular old **businessman.**
oyaji wa futsū ni **rīman** yatteru
親父は普通にリーマンやってる。

Office lady
ōeru
OL

I'm just a regular old **office lady.**
atashi wa futsū no **ōeru** nano
あたしは普通の**OL**なの。

••••• Everyday people
ippan pī
一般ピー

In America you have your stoners, preppies, hipsters, band geeks, jocks, goths, visigoths, rednecks, punks, computer nerds, ravers, art kids, and those student government types who end up banging your wife later on in life. Likewise, Japan has its own set of stock characters that you will learn to recognize. So take this book and a pair of binoculars and see if you can identify the following Japanese archetypes:

c PŪTARŌ OR FURĪTĀ
プー太郎 OR フリーター

A *pūtarō* or *furītā* is a Japanese Generation X'er. These are kids in their twenties who have graduated from college but, reluctant to become a cog in the corporate machinery, take part-time jobs at the local 7-Eleven and spend their paychecks on clothes and cell phone accessories. *Furītā* are treated as a big social problem, on a par with drugs and violence, but really they're just your average college grads with nothing better to do than piss off Mom by drinking milk straight out of the carton. They check their e-mail like fifty times an hour and are really into the Food Network.

‹ GYARU ギャル

This is one of the more notorious Japanese archetypes. Girls with overwrought tans, blond hair, bright fluorescent clothing, and white glitter makeup around their eyes. There are different levels of *gyaru*, the most violent manifestation of which is the *yamamba*, whose tan is so dark and whose eye makeup is so garishly white that under the black light of a dance club she appears to be a pair of disembodied raccoon eyes. As a foreigner, you may be inclined to make fun of *gyaru*, and Japanese people often act ashamed of them, but they are actually more fun to party with than just about anybody. Think of them as Japanese Jersey girls! They dance, drink, and know how to get dirty—so hang up your hang-ups and go hit up Shibuya for a good, peroxide-tinted time. *Gyaru banzai*!

‹ BURIKKO ぶりっ子

A ditz. Literally, *burikko* mean "a girl who pretends." Like her American counterpart, a *burikko* isn't actually ditzy, per se—she just pretends to be because her dad molested her as a kid and she assumed feigned ignorance as a primitive defense mechanism. And she thinks dudes actually like Paris Hilton. She's actually really sharp, and says some funny shit when you get her drunk enough—but then when you start to get intimate and ask her for her number she'll suddenly clam up and say: "You mean, like, my social security number?!"

‹ YANKĪ ヤンキー

A bastardization of the word "yankee," *yankī* refers to the male version of *gyaru*. Like *gyaru*, they tend to have long blond hair and obsessive tans, and are likewise undereducated. Don't hate on them for looking a little froufrou, though—these guys are the blue-collar workers of Japan, building Tokyo's skyscrapers by day and sniffing paint thinner by night. They are also tons more fun to rap with than your average salaryman, and can hold their own in a fight if it comes down to it. Same story as *gyaru*, basically, without a vagina.

⊂ OTAKU オタク

Otaku is a word that, like *bukkake*, has insinuated itself into the English language. These are the guys who spend all night in their apartment with the lights out, playing World of Warcraft and jerking off to science fiction *anime*. This is not a judgmental description: in my opinion these folks deserve our awe and our reverence. They have the balls to do what your ego and pride will never allow you to do—sink into the mire of self-indulgence, without any regard for what society might say. So next time an *otaku* walks by you on his way to the video arcade, stop for a moment, take off your hat, and hum the intro to Final Fantasy, in the slightly wavering key of hesitant admiration.

⊂ HKKĪ ヒッキー

Hikkī are a relatively new phenomenon in Japan. A particularly acute manifestation of the *furītā* generation, a *hikkī* is like a violent amalgam of otaku and apathy. *Hikkī* stay in their rooms all day, so afraid of societal pressure that their lethargy actually becomes an active commitment on a par with a full-time job. The word *hikkī* can also refer to Japanese pop singer Utada Hikaru, but in this case it is short for *hikikomori*, which means "to hole up."

⊂ AKIBAKEI アキバ系

A-Boy These anime fanatics are essentially *otaku*, but encompass a slightly larger and more colorful demographic. Akiba refers to Akihabara, the electronics/anime mecca of Tokyo (and the world at large). So basically *akiba kei* means the kind of people that hang out in Akihabara. This includes folks who like to dress up as their favorite anime characters (cosplay), computer enthusiasts, hard-core gamers, and the just plain socially awkward. Sometimes referred to as "A-Boys"—a pun on the term B-Boys.

⊂ BĪBŌI ビーボーイ

B-boy This is a jigger. Not like when Jay-Z says "Jigga that Nigga" or when your grandpa asks you to fetch him "a jigger of gin"—no, this is the Japanese version of a "wigger": a Japanese boy who thinks that every day is Halloween and his only costume is an Eminem outfit. You can find groups of jiggers break-dancing to Jamiroquai in subway stations throughout Japan. Not as lame as their Caucasian counterparts but still pretty ridiculous, *bībōi* wear Kangol hats and Timberline boots but would probably turn tail at the very sight of a Paki dude, much less a real black guy. Flash them a gang sign and then get all tripped out when *they actually flash a gang sign back.*

⊂ RĪMAN リーマン

salaryman This is perhaps the most pervasive demographic in Tokyo—the ubiquitous, expressionless businessman. The weird thing about these dudes is that you can get drunk with them and see them emerge from their elaborate cocoons of mannerism, spread their powdery wings and ascend unto the sky, laughing and singing and shitting on their bosses and wives and the whole sham of modern life—only to glance at their watches and say, "Oh shit, I'm gonna miss the last train."

‹ ŌERU OL

OL stands for "office lady." This is basically the adult manifestation of the Japanese schoolgirl—now that she has graduated from college, she is working in an office until she gets knocked up. On weekends she goes to Disneyland with her boyfriend and throws a fit when his eyes are closed in the twenty-dollar Splash Mountain photo. She is lousy in bed.

‹ BABĀ ババア

Middle-aged ladies. Soccer moms. In the United States, the demographic of middle-aged women either have this erotic Desperate Housewives appeal to them, or else they serve as an antidote to the boner you seem to get in class every day at 2:00 p.m. In Japan, middle-aged ladies gravitate toward the latter, with all the spite and zealotry of evangelism thrown in. Remember that one friend you had in high school, whose mom hated you because she somehow *knew* that you were getting her son high? Remember how she called all your other friends' moms and got them to hate you, too? Yeah, well picture that, but riding a motor scooter at 50 mph through Japanese suburbia. Not to be fucked with.

CHAPTER 3

PARTY JAPANESE

WAIWAI NIHONGO
わいわい日本語

••••Let's party
asobō
遊ぼう

If you think about it, partying has a lot to do with slang. When you loosen your tie after a hard day's work, you have the opportunity to loosen up your tongue as well. That's why the best places to hear and speak Japanese slang are clubs and drinking establishments.

‹ ARE YOU UP FOR...
. . .ittoku
…いっとく？

. . .some karaoke?
karaoke. . .
カラオケ…

. . .another drink?
mō ippai. . .
もういっぱい…

. . .staying out all night?
ōru. . .
オール…

. . .another rail?
rain, mō ippon. . .
ライン、もう一本…

< C'MON, LET'S…
shiyōze. . .
…しようぜ？

…do something!
nanka. . .
何か…

…drink at my house!
orenchi de nomikai. . .
俺んちで飲み会…

…play a drinking game!
nomi gēme. . .
飲みゲーム…

…do some partying!
tonikaku asobu koto ni. . .
とにかく遊ぶことに…

…raise the roof!
iei iei. . .
イエイイエイ…

…take it easy tonight.
kon'ya wa mattari. . .
今夜はまったり…

…hit on some guys.
gyaku nan. . .
逆ナン…

...hit on some girls.
nanpa...
ナンパ…

...smoke some weed and shit.
happa suttari...
ハッパ吸ったり…

...take a break.
chotto kyūkei ni...
ちょっと休憩に…

‹ I WANNA...
...tai na
…たいな

...meet some new people.
atarashī tomodachi tsukuri...
新しい友達作り…

...go somewhere else.
hoka no tokoro itte mi...
他のところ行ってみ…

...blow this pop stand.
koko o dete iki...
ここを出て行き…

...score a man.
otoko o kudoki...
男を口説き…

...score a woman.
onna o kudoki...
女を口説き…

...go home early.
hayaku kaeri...
早く帰り…

·····Whatcha up to?
ima nani shiteru?
今何してる？

Whatcha up to?
ima nani shiteru
今何してる？

Are you busy tonight?
kon'ya isogashī
今夜忙しい？

I'm totally bored stupid.
maji chō hima dayo
マジ超ヒマだよ。

Whatcha wanna do?
dō suru
どうする？

I dunno... What you wanna do?
ūn dō suru
ううん．．．どうする？

Anyway, let's party.
tonikaku asobō
とにかく遊ぼう。

Bring it on!
yosshā
よっしゃー！

·····Getting down
nori nori
ノリノリ

Do you want to know what is the single sexiest thing about somebody you meet at a club—the essential element that sets them apart from every other piece of tail on the dance floor? *The fact that they are having a good time.* You wanna be sexy? Then have a good time, dammit—right now! Then tell everybody about it, using the following phrases:

‹ TONIGHT I...
...kon'ya wa
…今夜は

...am in the mood to party!
...nori nori daze
…ノリノリだぜ

...am getting my groove on.
...nori ni notteru
…ノリにノッてる。

...am ready for anything.
...yaru ki manman
…やる気満々。

...am having a great time!
...moriagatteru
…盛り上がってる。

...will take this party higher!
...tenshon o dondon ageru zo
…テンションをどんどん上げるぞ。

...will stay up all night.
...ōru suru zo
…オールするぞ。

••••• Taking it easy
mattari
まったり

Not every night can be a party night. That's why they have Blockbuster nights. Actually, in Japan they would be called "Tsutaya nights"—if they weren't already called *mattari*. So go get a romantic comedy and a bucket of green tea ice cream, wiggle under the *kotatsu*, and have yourself a good *mattari*.

‹ TONIGHT I. . .
kon'ya wa. . .
今夜は…

. . .am beat.
. . .darī na
…だりぃーな。

. . .don't feel like doing shit.
. . .nani mo shitakunē
…何もしたくねー。

. . .feel like taking it easy.
. . .mattari shitai kibun
…まったりしたい気分。

. . .am gonna eat and go to sleep.
. . .meshi kutte neru
…メシ食って寝る

. . .am just gonna veg out at home.
. . .ie de goro goro shiteru wa
…家でゴロゴロしてるわ。

. . .wanna watch videos or something.
. . .bideo demo mitai
…ビデオでも見たい。

·····Funny shit
ukeru koto
ウケること

In spite of the stereotype, Japanese folks have a great sense of humor. You're going to have plenty of shit to laugh about, so you might as well learn how to do it right:

<. . .IS/ARE HILARIOUS!
. . .mecha ukeru
…めちゃウケる！

His/her outfit. . .
aitsura no fukusō. . .
あいつの服装…

Everything you say. . .
omae no iu koto. . .
お前の言うこと…

His/her face. . .
aitsura no kao. . .
あいつの顔…

This movie. . .
kono eiga . . .
この映画…

The way you dance. . .
omae no odorikara. . .
お前の踊り方…

‹. . .MAKE(S) ME LOSE MY SHIT!
. . .waratchau
…笑っちゃう！

Just looking at them. . .
aitsura no kao o miru dake de. . .
あいつらの顔を見るだけで…

Your stupid jokes. . .
omae no kudaranai gyagu. . .
お前の下らないギャグ…

They always. . .
aitsura no koto wa itsumo. . .
あいつらのことはいつも…

▪▪▪▪▪Cool shit
omoroi koto
おもろいこと

Omoroi is your all-purpose word for interestingness. You can use it to describe how funny it was when your friend got drunk and fell into a sewer ditch, or how enamored you are by the music of David Hasselhoff, or how you were moved by an exhibit at the Hiroshima War Memorial. Anything you find appealing is *omoroi*. When the moon hits your eye like a big pizza pie, that's *omoroi*.

c FUNNY / COOL / FASCINATING

omoroi
オモロい

This movie is **great**.
kono eiga **omoroi** nā
この映画、**オモロ**いなー。

Japanese folks are **funny**.
nihonjin tte **omoroi** yone
日本人って、**オモロ**いよね。

Take me somewhere **fun**.
dokka **omoroi** toko ni tsuretette
どっか**オモロ**いとこに連れてって。

Do you know any **cool** clubs?
dokka **omoroi** kurabu shiranai
どっか**オモロ**いクラブ知らない？

That's one **funky** hairdo.
sono kamigata kanari **omoroi** ne
その髪型、かなり**オモロ**いね。

You are a real **fun** kid.
anta **omoroi** ko dane
あんた、**オモロ**い子だね。

·····Where Japanese people get down
日本人の遊び方

Nihonjin no asobikata

Japanese kids don't go to "bars." Actually, they do—just not as often as they go to other places, like karaoke or clubs. Here's a list of different ways that Japanese folks get stupid:

ᴄ IZAKAYA 居酒屋

The standard Japanese drinking establishment. It's basically a cross between a bar and a restaurant. Most of your drinking will be done in one of these.

That **izakaya** has shitty food but the drinks are cheap.
asoko no **izakaya** wa meshi ga mazui kedo sake ga yasui kara
あそこの居酒屋は飯がまずいけど酒が安いから。

ᴄ KARAOKE カラオケ

Small, private karaoke rooms rented by the hour.

Yesterday we sang every Beatles song in the **karaoke** joint.
kinō wa **karaoke** de bītoruzu no zenkyoku utatte shimatta
昨日はカラオケでビートルズの全曲歌ってしまった。

ᴄ KURABU クラブ

Loud music and drinks. Often categorized by the type of music being DJed: Hip-hop club, Reggae club, Punk club.

Do you know a good **club** for picking up rich, handsome men?
kanemochi no ikemen o getto dekisō na **kurabu** shitteru
金持ちのイケメンをゲットできそうなクラブ知ってる？

ᴄ GĒSEN ゲーセン

A video game arcade. Swallow your pride, man—nothing beats a good game of drunken Tekken.

Last night I got so drunk I wound up playing Dance Dance Revolution at the **arcade.**
kinō wa nomisugite **gēsen** de danrebo nanka yatchattā
昨日は飲みすぎてゲーセンでダンレボなんかやっちゃったー。

ᴄ FAMIRESU ファミレス

Short for "family restaurant," this implies Denny's or some other chain restaurant. They have much better food than their American counterparts and serve alcohol! Often open 24 hours, for when a night gets really sloppy.

Let's wait for the first train at a **family restaurant.**
famiresu de asaichi no densha o matō
ファミレスで朝一の電車を待とう。

⊂ MANGA KISSA 漫画喫茶

A twenty-four-hour Internet café/comic book library. Pay by the hour to read, watch movies, obsessively frag, send drunken mass e-mails, or just sleep until the morning train. Not a party place, per se, but a good place to kill time between parties. Free soft drinks.

There's nothing to do till the club opens up—wanna hit up a **manga kissa?**
kurabu ga aku made yarukoto nai kara **manga kissa** demo ittemiru
クラブが開くまでやることないから漫画喫茶で
もいってみる？

⊂ BĀ, NOMIYA バー・飲み屋

A Western-style bar, specializing in alcohol rather than food.

⊂ SUNAKKU スナック

A bar with flirty waitresses. Middle-aged dudes love these places, but they charge you up the yin-yang for a half-assed cocktease.

⊂ HOSUTESU KURABU ホス テスクラブ

An expensive bar with younger girls who will drink with you and sometimes more, depending on your wallet and your demeanor.

‹ HOSUTESU KURABU ホストクラブ

Ladies, don't feel objectified! You, too, can pay to drink with handsome young men who might even chomp your box for a nominal fee!

‹ SUTORIPPU ストリップ

A titty bar.

‹ NOMIKAI 飲み会

A party.

Usually takes place at an *izakaya* (see page 46).

‹ ENKAI 宴会

Same as *nomikai*, but usually celebrating a specific thing.

‹ HANAMI 花見

Spread out a picnic blanket beneath the cherry blossoms, and watch everyone proceed to drink until said picnic blanket is a kaleidoscopic Jackson Pollock of chunder.

‹ DONKĪ ドンキー

Welcome to Don Quixote, the Japanese Wal-Mart. Not a place you want to go party at, but it's open 24 hours and you can always find some interesting folks wandering the aisles at 3 a.m.

‹ NIJIKAI 二次会

The after party. This can be held at any of the above establishments, and often involves missing your train, puking on your friend's shoes, and hitting on nameless coworkers.

‹ GŌKON / KOMPA 合コン・コンパ

A dude invites his male friends, and a girl invites her female friends, and everybody gets drunk and feels each other out. At some point the girls go to the bathroom and decide who gets who. Basically it's an institutionalized version of Friday night at the bar.

⟨ ŌRU オール

This means "Fuck the last train, we're drinking till morning," and it happens more often than not.

⟨ YAMANOTE SEN GĒMU 山手線ゲーム

A drinking game where you go around in a circle and say the names of stations on the Yamanote Line. When somebody fucks up, they drink. There are a million other themes for this, like the names of prefectures or names of foreign actresses.

⟨ ŌSAMA GĒMU 王様ゲーム

This is basically the Japanese equivalent of "Truth or Dare." Kind of childish and dumb, unless you're drunk enough that it's right on your level.

ᐧᐧᐧᐧᐧBooze
sake
酒

Bacchus has his own language. Mostly it consists of slurred confessions about how much you love your friends, but there are other Bacchanalian vocabules that you won't be embarrassed of the next morning:

⟨ CHEERS TO. . . !
ni kampai
… に乾杯！

...this **beautiful country!**
kono **utsukushī kuni**...
この美しい国 …

. . .the **kindness** of Japanese people!
nihonjin no **shinsetsusa**. . .
日本人の親切さ…

. . .recovering from **alcoholism!**
aruchū ga naotta koto. . .
アル中が治ったこと …

. . .all my **ex-wives** (husbands)!
mototsuma (motodanna) tachi. . .
元妻（元旦那）たち …

. . .**brew!**
mugishu. . .
麦酒…

How about **a drink**?
ippai ikaga
一杯いかが？

You got **beer on tap?**
nama bīru arimasuka
生ビールありますか？

"Beer on tap" in Japan implies a light pilsner.

A **pint of beer**, please.
namachū kudasai
生中ください

Namachū is the standard beer order—a medium-sized
(pint) glass from the tap.

Know somewhere we can drink a **microbrew?**
dokka **jibīru** nomeru mise wakaru
どっか地ビール飲める店わかる？

You probably need to go up into the mountains, to a hot
spring or ski resort, to find a good microbrew.

I want to learn more about **saké.**
ponshu ga motto kuwashiku naritai
ポン酒がもっと詳しくなりたい。

Ponshu is short for *nipponshu*, or "Japanese booze." The word *sake* tends to be a general term for booze.

Hot saké gets me fucked up, man.
atsukan wa mechakucha yō kara na
熱燗はめちゃくちゃ酔うからな。

Astukan is heated saké, usually drunk in the winter, and usually cheaper than the drler saké you drink cold.

Why don't you **shotgun** that saké?
soko no ponshu o **ikkinomi** shitara
そこのポン酒を一気飲みしたら？

There's not a lot of beer-bonging in Japan, but you do get a lot of good old-fashioned chugging.

Chug! Chug! Chug!
ikki ikki ikki
一気一気一気！

This is what you yell while people chug chug chug.

Let's drink until the **last train.**
shūden made nomō ze
終電まで飲もうぜ。

…which ain't all that late in Tokyo.

I'm gonna drink till it **comes back up!**
ribāsu suru made nomu dē
リバースするまで飲むでー。

Hilariously enough, they call puking "reversing."

If you're going to **barf**, do it in the toilet.
gero tchaunnara toire de yare
ゲロっちゃうんならトイレでやれ。

ᐸ OTHER DRINKS THAT JAPANESE PEOPLE ENJOY:

Shōchū (potato liquor—drunk by the pros)
焼酎。

Chūhai (a cocktail with *shōchū*)
酎ハイ。

((((((((((A DRINKING SONG))))))))))))
NOMIUTA 飲み歌

Ra-ra-raccoon balls, see them sway
Even on a windless day
And when Papa Raccoon spied
These balls he laughed till he cried
And his own balls swung side to side.

tan tan tanuki no kintama wa
kaze mo nai noni yura yura
sore o miteita oya danuki
hara o kakaete wa hha hha
chōshi o awasete yura yura

たんたん たぬきの金玉は
風もないのに ゆらゆら
それを見ていた 親だぬき
腹をかかえて わっはっはっ
調子を合わせて ゆらゆら

⸱⸱⸱⸱⸱Fucked-up-edness
deisui
泥酔

Whatever, man—you aren't going to remember any of these vocabulary words when you're sprawled out on the *tatami* mats breathing fire. But I guess maybe this will make for some nice hangover retrospection as you sit there trying to remember what happened last night.

⊂ I'M STARTING TO GET...
...shite kichatta
…してきちゃった。

...buzzed.
horoyoi...
ほろ酔い…

...a little **tipsy**—oh no!
yabai chotto **fura fura**...
ヤバい、ちょっとフラフラ…

...a bit **drunk.**
yopparatta kanji ga...
酔っぱらった感じが…

...**sick.**
hakike...
吐き気…

⊂ I AM...
...ni nattekita
…になってきた。

...smashed.
beron beron...
べろんべろん…

...really **trashed.**
mō **guden guden**...
もうぐでんぐでん…

. . .three sheets to the wind.
chō deisui jyōtai. . .
超泥酔状態…

Yesterday I got so **smashed** I was hitting on girls in the train.
kinō nanka **beron beron** ni natte densha no naka de nanpa shimakuri
昨日なんか、べろんべろんになって電車の中でナンパしまくり。

Don't try talking to him—he's already **three sheets to the wind.**
aitsu wa mō **chō deisui jyōtai** nanode hanashi kakenai hō ga ī ze
あいつはもう**超泥酔状態**なので話しかけない方がいいぜ。

Yesterday I totally **drunk-dialed** my own sister.
kinō sa jibun no ane ni **yopparatte denwa** nanka kakechimatta
昨日さ、自分の姉に酔っぱらって電話なんかかけちまった。

Hi, my name's Nancy, and I'm an **alcoholic.**
konnichiwa watashi wa nanshī to īmasu aru chū desu
こんにちは、私はナンシーと言います、アル中です。

••••• Weed
happa
ハッパ

If you've been in Japan for more than a couple days, you've probably noticed an elementary school kid or middle-aged lady sporting a marijuana-emblazoned T-shirt. This doesn't mean that said woman or child is down with the 420. On the contrary, it probably means that they have no idea what bud is. This is how pot works in Japan: you don't talk about it except with folks who do it. Kind of like swinging in America. Anyway, there are plenty of people in Japan who enjoy a puff before a night on the town, and quite a few who enjoy more puffs than that. One caveat, though: outside of Hokkaido, Japanese weed is *really* bad—and I don't just say that because I'm from Oregon. Especially in Tokyo, you usually wind up with this turdy black hash that looks and smokes like some hippie just scraped it out of his homemade Fimo pipe. Note: Not to harsh anyone's stony mellow, but the laws in Japan in regard to possession and distribution of bud is not friendly. So follow your natural sense of paranoia when smoking.

What do Japanese folks think about **marijuana?**
nihonjin wa **marifana** ni tsuite dō omotteiru
日本人は**マリファナ**についてどう思っている？

I heard that **bud** grows wild up in Hokkaido.
hokkaido de wa **taima** ga shizen ni haeru tte kītandakedo
北海道では**大麻**が自然に生えるって聞いたんだけど。

You know where I can get some **trees** around here?
dokka **kusa** ga te ni hairu tokoro wakaru
どっか**９３**が手に入るところわかる？

Don't you have anything other than **hash?**
choko igai no mono wa nai no
チョコ以外のものはないの？

I didn't bring a **piece.**
paipu motte kitenai wa
パイプ持ってきてないわ。

Wanna take some **bong** rips?
baburā de suttee miyō ka
バブラーで吸ってみようか？

I'm getting a little **stoned.**
chotto **raritte** kita na
ちょっと**ラリ**ってきたな。

Shit, I'm **really fucking baked.**
yabai ore **itchatte iru** wa
やばい、俺、**イッ**ちゃっているわ。

Check him out—he's **stoned out of his mind.**
hora aitsu **raripappa** nandaze
ほら、あいつ**ラリパッパ**なんだぜ。

I've **got the munchies** something fierce.
ore wa kanari **manchitteru**
俺はかなり**マンチ**ってる。

·····Coke
kōku
コーク

They do have cocaine in Japan, I guess. At least you often
hear folks talking about it. You also see news reports about
wayward cops dealing it and celebrities getting pulled over
with blow all over their dashboard—just like in America! So,
for what it's worth, here's my understanding of *Scarface*
parlance as it is spoken in contemporary Tokyo.

You know where I can get me some of that **white powder?**
shiroi kona ga te ni hairu toko wakaru
白い粉が手に入るトコわかる？

Cut me up a big, fat **line.**
omoikkishi futē **rain** o hītoite kure
思いっきしふてぇー**ライン**を引いといてくれ。

Let's go into the bathroom for **a bump.**
chotto toire itte **snitte** kukka
ちょっとトイレ行って**スニ**ってくっか？

I'm not going to be in Japan long, so I don't need you to
hook me up with a **dealer.**
nihon ni wa nagaku iru tsumori wa nainde **bainin** no shōkai
wa iranai
日本には長くいるつもりはないんで、**売人**の紹
介はいらない。

Are all Japanese comedians on **coke?**
nihon no owarai san wa minna **kōku** yatten'no
日本のお笑いさんはみんな**コーク**やってんの？

CHAPTER 4

BODY JAPANESE
体に関する日本語

••••• The Japanese ideal
nihonjin no risō
日本人の理想

The Japanese ideal is a little different than the American ideal, but probably not all that different. I mean, in Africa they like girls with elongated labia, and in Europe I've heard it's cool for guys to wear those weenie soccer shoes.

> **‹ HE/SHE HAS...**
> kare/kanojo wa...
> 彼・彼女は…
>
> **. . .a small head**
> . . .atama ga chīsai
> …頭が小さい
>
> **. . .a slender face**
> . . .kao ga hosoi
> …顔が細い

57

. . .round eyes
…kurikuri me
…くりくり目

. . .a short torso and long legs
…dōtan chōsoku
…胴短長足

. . .a good figure
…sutairu ga ī
…スタイルがいい

⊂ HE/SHE IS...
kare/kanojo wa. . .
彼・彼女は…

. . .cute (guys and girls, but mostly girls)
…kawaī
…かわいい

. . .pretty (girls)
…kirei
…きれい

. . .beautiful (girls)
…utsukushī
…美しい

. . .hot (guys) **or cool** (girls)
…kakko ī
…カッコイイ

. . .stylish
…oshare
…おしゃれ

. . .popular with the opposite sex
…mote mote
…モテモテ

. . .hip
…iketeru
…イケてる

. . .slim
…surarito shiteiru
…すらりとしている

. . .skinny
. . .hosoi
…細い

. . .clean/kempt
. . .sappari shiteiru
…っぱりしている

·····The Japanese ugly
nijon no busaiku
日本の「ぶさいく」

ᑕ HE/SHE HAS A...
kare/kanojo wa. . .
彼・彼女は…

. . .big head
. . .atama ga ōkī
…頭が大きい

. . .round face
. . .kao ga marui
…顔が丸い

. . .narrow eyes
. . .kitsune me
…狐目

. . .long torso and short legs
. . .dōnaga tansoku
…胴長短足

. . .bad figure
. . .sutairu ga warui
…スタイルが悪い

⊂ HE/SHE IS...
kare/kanojo wa...
彼・彼女は…

. . .ugly (guys and girls)
. . .busaiku
…ぶさいく

. . .ugly (girl)
. . .busu
…ぶす

. . .ugly (guy)
. . .gesu
…げす

. . .lame
. . .dasai
…ださい

. . .unpopular with the opposite sex
. . .motenai
…モテない

. . .unhip
. . .iketenai
…イケてない

. . .husky
. . .kobutori
…小太り

. . .chubby
. . .potchari
…ぽっちゃり

. . .fat
. . .debu
…でぶ

. . .chunky
. . .debuccho
…でぶっちょ

. . .dirty/disheveled
. . .kitanai
…汚い

⊂ OTHER BODY TYPES:

HE/SHE IS...
kare/kanojo wa. . .
彼・彼女は…

. . .little (not just height—altogether small)
. . .kogara
… 小柄

. . .ripped
. . .gottsui
…ごっつい

. . .delicate
. . .kyasha
…華奢

. . .tanned
. . .hiyake shiteiru
…日焼けしている

. . .pale
. . .aojiroi
…青白い

. . .scrawny
. . .gari gari shiteiru
…ガリガリしている

. . .hunched over (bad posture)
. . .nekoze
…猫背

. . .short
. . .chibikko
…ちびっこ

. . .hairy
. . .kemoja
…毛もじゃ

Looks like you're getting a bit of a **beer belly** there.
chotto **bīruppara** ga dekita mitai dane
ちょっとビールっぱらができたみたいだね。

I gotta go on a **diet**.
daietto shinakya
ダイエットしなきゃ。

Japanese people have **square asses**.
nihonjin wa **ketsu ga shikakui**
日本人はケツは四角い。

Check out my **sixpack**!
hora **fukkin wareteru** daro
ほら、腹筋割れてるだろ！

I need to shave my **bikini line**.
bikini rain o soranakya
ビキニラインを剃らなきゃ。

Man, you are totally **ripped**!
omae **kin'niku mori mori** jan
お前、筋肉モリモリじゃん！

·····Piss
shonben
小便

If you're ever looking for someplace to drink in Tokyo, there's a creepy chain of bars called Seiryūmon where, if you go in the men's room and stand in front of the urinal, it starts laughing at you, and then the urinal *actually starts moving around* so that you have to really make a concerted effort to grip and aim if you don't want to piss all over your new Japanese shoes.

I wanna go **pee**.
oshikko shitai
おしっこしたい。

I gotta take a **leak**.
shonben shitē
小便してぇー。

I am experiencing an **urge to make urine**.
nyōi ga sashite mairimashita
尿意がさして参りました。

Lets **piss together!**
tsureshon shiyō ze
連れションしようぜ！

I **pissed** all over my hands.
te ni shonben o kakechatta
手に小便をかけちゃった。

I am a pathetic **bed wetter**.
watashi wa shō mo nai **onesho** desu
私はしようもないオネショです。

Check out that drunk businessman **pissing in public!**
hora yopparai rīman ga **tachishon** shiteru
ほら、酔っぱらいリーマンが立ちションしてる！

·····Shit
kuso
くそ

Personally, I think that poo is pretty funny. Farting is funnier, but poo is pretty damn hilarious. So I must say that I was deeply disappointed to find that the average Japanese person really isn't that entertained by dookie. They just don't have the weird Judeo-Christian taboo about excretion that makes it so funny to us. You can take a Japanese girl on a first date to an expensive Italian restaurant and she will gaze at you over the candles and flowers and Château Duchebage and say, "I've got mad diarrhea today"—AND IT WON'T BE FUNNY. Trust me, it took me a *lot* of failed potty talk to learn this lesson. Play your giggles off like you're just about to sneeze or something.

I need to **poop.**
unko shitai
うんこしたい。

I gotta take a **dump.**
kuso shitē
くそしてぇー。

I've got **nasty diarrhea.**
yabai geri shiteru
ヤバいゲリしてる。

I'm **peeing out my ass** today.
kyō wa **geripī** shitemāsu
今日はゲリピーしてまーす。

I'm been super **constipated** lately.
saikin wa mecha **bempi** de sā
最近はめちゃ便秘でさあ。

Check out the **curlicue turd!** *
hora **makiguso** ga aru do
ほら、まきぐそがあるど！

* The curlicue turd is a sort of icon in modern Japan. It looks like the picture above.

Don't forget to **wipe.**
fuku no o wasurezu ni na
拭くのを忘れずにな。

Dude, you smell like **crap.**
omae **unchi** kusē na
おまえ、うんちくせーな。

You're such a **dung beetle.**
kono **funkorogashi**
この糞転がし！

"Dung beetle" is a really funny word in Japanese because it literally means "poop-roller"—in other words, somebody who pushes these big balls of turd around all day.

Sorry man, I just dropped a pretty **stinky duce.**
sakki **kanari kusai unchi** shichattandakedo gomen na
さっきかなりくさいうんちしちゃったんだけ
ど、ごめんな。

••••• Farts
onara
おなら

You couldn't pick a better language to fart in than Japanese. This is because Japanese has a lot of onomatopoeia—words that represent sounds. But before we get to the action fart sounds, let's get the basics down:

Who **farted!**
onara shita no wa doitsu da
オナラしたのはどいつだ！

I just cut **the cheese.**
he koichimatta de
屁こいちまったで。

Why do I so relish the **smell** of my own farts?
jibun no onara no **nioi** ga kon'nanimo konomashī no wa naze de arō
自分のオナラの臭いがこんなにも好ましいのは
なぜであろう。

Somebody must have **let one slip.**
dareka ga **morashitanda** na
誰かが**漏らしたんだ**な。

Damn, you're like a **suicide** bomber with your gas today!
yabē omae kyō wa **jibaku tero** no yō na onara da na
やべー、お前、今日は**自爆テロ**のようなオナラ
だな！

⊂ SPECIALTY FARTS

Somebody was pulling some nasty **one-cheek sneaks**
during that meeting.
dareka ga kaigichū ni yabē **sukashippe** o morashiteta
誰かが会議中にヤべえ**すかしっ屁**を漏らして
た。

The word *sukashippe*（すかしっ屁）literally means
"transparent fart," and roughly corresponds to the English
"silent-but-violent" or "one-cheek sneak." The lady next to
you on the airplane is an expert at them.

And for your present I got you... **a cup of tea!**
hai kimi no purezento wa **nigirippe** dā
はい、君のプレゼントは・・・**にぎりっ屁**だあ！

An integral part of Japanese etiquette, the *nigirippe*（にぎ
りっ屁）involves farting into your hand and then carrying
the fart into the proximity of a friend's nose before unfurling
your fingers and asking, in a smarmy British accept, "Cup
o' tea, gov'ner?"

Somebody just pulled a **drive-by** on us!
aitsu ni he no **morashinige** sarechimatta
あいつに屁の**漏らし逃げ**されちまった！

This is pretty self-explanatory. Also known as a "hit-and-
run," this is when you fart right before getting off an elevator
or leaving a room. The sheer cowardice of the act leaves a
sour enough smell in the air.

**Below are several examples of classic Japanese fart
noises.** Each of these words has its own unique meaning
and lyrical value. Try saying them out loud in order to really

feel what kinds of fart they stand for. Then feel kind of weird for farting with your mouth.

I just let...
...tte onara shita
…ってオナラした！

. . .a healthy, bubbly fart
buri buri...
ぶりぶり…

. . .a fluffier, loofah fart
bufu...
ぶふ…

. . .the classic, enunciated fart
pū...
ぷー…

‹ BUSUN
ぶすん

bu is the sound of the initial pop, while *sun* portrays the subsequent hiss. So it's like the dike breaks, and then the water flows out.

⊂ BUĪ
ぶいー

Pronounced "bwweee," it's one of those farts where you try to play it off like a stomach-whistle but then you realize that you've totally fumed the room.

⊂ SUKĀ
すかー

A whisperer. See *sukashippe* above.

⊂ SUSU
すす

The double whisper, for when it takes two puffs to blow out the candle in your pants.

⊂ BŌ
ぼー

A rumbler. Like when you're sitting in a wooden chair and the gas is just whapping out of your ass.

⊂ BERI BERI
べりべり

Like *buriburi* above, but wetter. Pasty.

⊂ PUKYŪ
ぷきゅー

A tight, well-pronounced fart. No legs are lifted, but rather the fart is pressed through the cheeks like pasta.

⊂ BUBIN
ぶびん

The octave. One of those farts that begins as a deep rumble but quickly crescendos into a falsetto snap.

In Japan, the blame for bad gas falls on the consumption of potatoes rather than beans. Namely, sweet potatoes. They are said to give one's gut a particularly good carbonating.

But farting feels good—and if it's good to you, it's good for you, as the old Japanese proverb says:

One fart is worth a thousand doses of medicine.
he hitotsu wa kusuri senpuku ni mukau.
屁一つは薬の千服に向かう。

••••• Snot / boogers / etc.
hanamizu / hanakuso / sonota
鼻水・鼻くそ・その他

Perhaps you noticed that the Japanese word for "booger" (hanakuso 鼻くそ) is just a compound of the word for "nose" and the word for "shit." Put them together, and you got "noseshit." Likewise, the words for "earwax" and "eyegunk" (also introduced in this section) are compound words for "earshit" and "eyeshit" respectively.

Hey, stop **picking your nose.**
kora **hana hojiru** na
こら、鼻ほじるな。

Don't just stand there with **snot** coming out your nose.
hana tarashitenjanēyo
洟垂らしてんじゃねーよ。

Dude, don't wipe your **boogers** on me!
oi jibun no **hanakuso** o hito ni tsukeru na yo
おい、自分の鼻くそを人につけるなよ！

I get most of my vitamins from **eating boogers.**
boku wa daitai **hanakuso o kutte** eiyō o totteirunda
僕はだいたい鼻くそを食って栄養をとっているんだ。

Don't you think this booger looks like **your mom?**
kono hanakuso **tte temē no kāchan** ni nitenē
この鼻くそって、**てめぇーの母ちゃん**に似てねー？

You got a **Kleenex?**
tisshu aru
ティッシュある？

I've got a **bloody nose.**
hanaji ga deta
鼻血が出た。

He was **covered in blood.**
aitsu wa **chimamire** datta
あいつは血まみれだった。

Check out this bountiful harvest of **earwax!**
mite kono **mimikuso** no hōfu na shūkaku
見て、この耳くその豊富な収穫！

You're sporting some mad **eyegunk.**
omae sugē **mekuso** ga tsuiteru
お前、すげー目くそがついてる。

Shit, I got a **zit** on my ass.
yabai ketsu ni **nikibi** ga dekita
やばい、ケツにニキビができた。

You should **pop** your zits, man.
omae nikibi o **tsubushita** hō ga ī zo
お前、ニキビを潰した方がいいぞ。

A shitload of **pus** came out!
sugē **umi** ga deta
すげーウミがでた！

I feel like **I'm gonna puke.**
hakike ga suru
吐き気がする。

I'm **puking** my guts out.
ore **gero o haki** makutteiru
俺、ゲロを吐きまくっている。

Last night I drank too much and **reversed** my dinner.
kinō wa nomisugite **ribāsu** shichatta
昨日は飲みすぎてリバースしちゃった。

I can still smell where he **drooled** on my pillow.
aitsu ga makura ni **yodare o tarashita** tokoro ga imada ni niō wa
あいつが枕に**ヨダレを垂らした**ところが未だに
臭うわ。

I could hear him **snoring** from outside!
aitsu no **ibiki** wa soto kara kikoerun damon
あいつの**イビキ**は外から聞こえるんだもん。

I dumped her because she **grinds her teeth** like crazy.
kanojo wa hidoi **hagishiri** suru kara wakareru koto ni
shitanda
彼女はひどい**歯ぎしり**するから別れることにし
たんだ。

Don't touch him, he has **cooties!**
aitsu wa **engacho** dakara fureru na
あいつは**エンガチョ**だから触れるな！

••••• Sickness
byōki
病気

When I first got to Japan, I was surprised to find that people
became uncomfortable when I told them about getting both
the clap and crabs in the same Canadian brothel. I guess the
Japanese are a little put off by the whole idea of Canada. But
they *are* very comfortable with talking about health issues,
so feel free to let everyone around you know just how rotten
you feel:

I feel gross.
kimochi warui
気持ち悪い。

I'm not **feeling good** lately.
saikin wa dōmo **taichō ga yokunai**
最近はどうも**体調がよくない**。

Dude, you **don't look so good.**
omae **kaoiro warui** zo
お前、**顔色悪いぞ**。

You're looking **pale**, there.
kao **aoi** zo
顔青いぞ。

You alright?
daijōbu kai
大丈夫かい？

That girl from the club gave me **the clap**.
kurabu no ko ni **rimbyō** o moratcchatta
クラブの子に淋病をもらっちゃった。

I think I caught a **cold**.
kaze o hīta kusai
風邪を引いたくさい。

I have a **stomachache**.
onaka itai
おなか痛い。

Looks like you ate **some bad** sushi.
osushi ni **atatta** mitai da
お寿司に当たったみたいだ。

I'm having my **period**.
ima wa **seirichū** nano
今は生理中なの。

I have pretty **heavy periods**.
atashi wa **seiri ga omoi** hō
あたしは生理が重い方。

I'm all **hung over** today.
kyō wa **futsukayoi** nanda
今日は二日酔いなんだ

I've got a **headache**.
zutsū ga suru
頭痛がする。

Call a **doctor**.
ishi o yobe
医師を呼べ。

Get me some **painkiller**.
itamidome o kure
痛み止めをくれ

CHAPTER 5

HORNY JAPANESE

ERO ERO NIHONGO

エロエロ日本語

·····Fucking
etchi

エッチ

No disrespect to the indigenous peoples of Canada or anything, but we English speakers have so many sundry and baroque idioms for "fucking" that it makes Inuits and their multitude of words for snow sound like a Speak & Spell that's running out of batteries. Likewise Japan has no shortage of idioms for dipping the old California Roll, depending on how obscure and offensive you want to get. So for brevity's sake what follows will be the "bare bones" of Japanese sexual parlance (and yes, that's a double entendre).

I'm getting in the mood to...
...ki ni natte kita

···気になってきた。

Let's go home and...
ie ni kaette ... koto ni shiyō
家に帰って…ことにしよう。

How 'bout it we...
...no wa dō
…のはどう？

All you ever do is...
...koto shika shinai na
…ことしかしないな。

...fuck
yaru...
やる…

...fuck like rabbits
yarimakuru...
やりまくる…

...get it on
etchi suru...
エッチする…

...have a quickie
ippatsu kamasu...
一発かます…

...hit that shit; bone
hameru...
ハメる…

...hump
omanko suru...
おまんこする…

•••••Genitalia, etc.
seiki nado
性器など

Remember how in high school you learned to sing "Head, Shoulders, Knees, and Toes" in Spanish? Remember playing a game of good old "Simon says touch your *cabeza*"? Turns out, this wasn't just lighthearted fun—professors of applied linguistics tell us that by touching the various parts of your body while saying their corresponding names out loud, you actually internalize a new language better. It's called "tactile learning," and I encourage you to try it with the following section. Simon says touch your *chimpoko*…

Touch my…
…sawatte
…触って。

Lick my…
…namete
…なめて。

Spank my…
…tataite
…叩いて。

Be gentle with my…
…teinei ni atsukatte
…丁寧に扱って。

Can I touch your…
…sawatte mo ī
…触ってもいい？

((((((((A THRONG OF DONGS))))))))
いろいろなチンコ

tiny dick	tanshō, tanchiin	短小、短チン
limp dick	fu'nyachin	フニャチン
big dick	dekachin	デカチン
huge cock	kyokon, kyochin	巨根、巨チン
hung like a horse	umanami	馬なみ

Can I lick your...
...namete mo ī
…舐めてもいい？

Can I spank your...
...tataite mo ī
…叩いてもいい？

Can I take a picture of your...
...no shashin o totte ī
…の写真を撮っていい？

Don't touch my...
...sawaru na
…触るな！

I love...
...daisuki
…大好き！

That is one (those are some) fantastic...
sore wa rippa na ... da
それは立派な…だ。

I've never seen a ... like that.
sonna ... mita koto nai
そんな…見たことない。

cock
chin chin
チンチン

Johnson
chinko
チンコ

dick
chimpo
チンポ

wiener
chimpoko
チンポコ

head
kitō
亀頭

the rim of the head
kari
カリ
(the chin, if you will—basically another word for the head)

nuts
tamatama
たまたま

nads
kintama
金玉

ballsack
fuguri
ふぐり

pubes (male)
chinge
チン毛

((((((((((A MESS OF BREASTS))))))))))
おっぱいがいっぱい

concave breasts	凹乳	otsu'nyū
breastless	無乳	mu'nyū
flat-chested	貧乳	hin'nyū
barely breasted	微乳	binyū
medium-breasted	中乳	chū'nyū
ample-breasted	豊乳	hō'nyū
big tits	巨乳	kyō'nyū
ginormous tits	爆乳	baku'nyū
beautiful tits	美乳	bi'nyū
fake tits	虚乳	kyo'nyū

mangina (male asshole)
ketsu manko
ケツマンコ

pussy
manko
マンコ

cunt
manman
マンマン

hairy pussy
kemeko
毛めこ

shaved pussy
paipan
パイパン

clit
kuri
栗

clit
mame
豆

G-spot
jī supo
Gスポ

pussy lips
bira bira
ビラビラ

tits
oppai
おっぱい

nipples
chikubi
乳首

nips
bī chiku
B地区

pubes (female)
mange
マン毛

pussy juice
aieki
愛液

ass
ketsu
ケツ

asshole
ketsu ana
ケツ穴

anus
anaru
アナル

perineum
ari no towatari
蟻の門渡り

(Literally, the Japanese word evokes a line of ants crawling out one hole, across a small patch of turf, and down into another, god bless them.)

····· Sexual acts
seikōi
性行為

You might not know what all these things mean in English, but that shouldn't stop you from learning them in Japanese. I mean, what better way to get acquainted with your own native "tongue" than by learning how to say "analingus" in Japanese?

I want to do some...
...ga shitai
…がしたい。

Wanna try...
...yatte miyō ka
…やってみようか？

Have you ever done...
...yatta koto aru
…やったことある？

I like...
...ga suki
…が好き。

I'm tired of...
...akite kita
…飽きてきた。

kissing
kisu
キス

petting
pettingu
ペッティング

dry-humping
sumata
素股

finger-banging
teman
手マン

cunnilingus
kunni
クンニ

fellatio
fera
フェラ

playing the skin flute
shakuhachi
尺八

swallowing
gokkun
ごっくん

facial
gansha
顔射

sitting on face
gammen kijō
顔面騎乗

sixty-nine
shikkusu nain
シックスナイン

titty-fucking
paizuri
パイズリ

missionary style
seijōi
正常位

doggy-style
bakku
バック

woman on top
kijōi
騎乗位

hard fucking
pisuton undō
ピストン運動
(literally: "piston motion")

threesome
sanpī
3 ピー

group sex
rankō
乱交

bondage
esu emu
SM

anal sex
anaru
アナル

sex on the rag
kechaman
ケチャマン
(literally, "ketchup pussy")

female ejaculation
shiofuki
潮吹き

scat
sukatoro
スカトロ

enema
kanchō
浣腸

golden shower
gammen shawā
顔面シャワー

bukkake (skeet skeet skeet)
bukkake
ぶっかけ
(If you don't know about *bukkake*, a uniquely Japanese kink until the World Wide Web globalized it, you probably haven't been watching enough Japanese porn. "Ceremonial cum drinking" doesn't really get the concept across. Google it if you must.)

Do it...
motto...
もっと…

. . .faster.
...hayaku
…早く

. . .slower.
...yukkuri
…ゆっくり

. . .harder.
…hageshiku
…激しく

. . .softer.
…yasashiku
…やさしく

. . .more.
…yatte
…やって

·····I'm coming!
iku iku!
いくいく！

Aside from "hello" and "goodbye," this will be the most useful Japanese phrase you ever learn—if you happen to be a highly attractive and outgoing individual with an indefatigable libido. Otherwise, you'll probably have to pull this book out mid-coitus and look the word up.

This hurts.
itaiwa
痛いわ。

This feels really good.
mecha kimochi ī
めちゃ気持ちいい！

I'm starting to get off.
kimochi yoku nattekita
気持ちよくなってきた。

I want to come.
ikitai
逝きたい。

I'm about to come.
ikisō
逝きそう。

I'm coming!
iku iku
逝く逝く！

Where do you want it?
doko ni hoshī
どこに欲しい？

Come in my ass!
ketsusha shite
ケツ射して！

I just came.
itchatta
逝っちゃった。

Do you have a...?
...aru
…ある？

Let's try using a...
...tsukatte miyō ka
…使ってみようか？

. . .condom
gomu. . .
ゴム…

. . .dildo
harigata. . .
張り型…

. . .double dildo
unagi. . .
うなぎ…

. . .bullet (egg) vibrator
pinku rōta. . .
ピンクローター…

. . .vibrator
baibu. . .
バイブ…

Do you like my fingers or your vibrator better?
ore no yubi to baibu to, dotchi ga ī?
俺の指とバイブと、どっちがいい？

I'm going to...
...shichau
…しちゃう。

I want to...
...shitai
…したい。

You won't...?
...shinai no
…しないの？

...get a hard-on
bokki...
勃起…

...have a wet dream
musei...
夢精…

...lob (have a half-boner)
handachi...
半起ち…

...beat off (male)
shiko shiko...
しこしこ…

...masturbate (male and female*)
onanī...
オナニー…

* Japanese lacks a mainstream slang word specific to female masturbation, though there's no shortage of private slang terms that groups of women use among themselves.

queef
manpe
マン屁

coming onto tits
paisha
パイ射

coming in an ass
ketsusha
ケツ射

c PEOPLE COME IN ALL SHAPES AND SIZES

People come in every color of the rainbow. People come in different sizes and shapes. People come in all sorts of people—at different speeds, with varying degrees of intensity, in an eclectic assortment of orifices, on any number of occasions, and employing a vast arsenal of manual and motorized tools. People make the world go round, is basically what I'm trying to say—so let's take a look at the different sorts of people that people come in.

I'm a bit of a… (female).
atashi chotto … nano
あたし、ちょっと…なの。

I'm a bit of a… (male).
ore … na tokoro ga arunda
俺、…なところがあるんだ。

You seem like a…
anta … ppoi na
あんた、…っぽいな。

Are you a…?
… nano
…なの？

slut
yariman
やりマン

cheap fuck
katsugaru
ケツ軽（尻軽）

lucky snatch
ageman
あげマン

(a woman who, when you sleep with her, makes your luck and general status in life change for the better)

unlucky snatch
sageman
さげマン
(a woman who, when you sleep with her, sucks all the luck out of you)

virgin
shojo
処女

dead fish
maguro
マグロ
(a girl who doesn't take an active role in lovemaking)

MILF
hitodzuma
人妻

bull dike
baritachi
バリタチ

lipstick lesbian
barineko
バリネコ

dirty whore
abazure
アバズレ

callgirl
kōrugāru
コールガール

player, pimp
yarichin
やりチン

quickdraw
mikosuri han
三こすり半
(premature ejaculator—literally, "three and a half strokes")

((((((((((LET'S HAVE A QUICKIE))))))))))
IPPATSU KAMASOU 一発かまそう

What is it, honey?
dōshita no dārin
どうしたのダーリン？

I'm feeling kinda horny.
etchi na kibun ni natchatta
エッチな気分になっちゃった

I want it now. I'm so horny.
ima hoshī. yokkyū ni natchauyō.
今ほしいー。欲求になっちゃうよー

For real? Here?
maji de? konna tokoro de?
まじで？こんなところで？

Yeah. Why not?
un. yoku nāai?
うん。よくなーーい？？

Alright then, get ready for some alley head.
jā. tachi kunni shite yaru.
じゃあ、立ちクンニしてやる

Ah! This is so embarrassing!
kya! hazui.
きゃ！ハズい

Damn, girl, you're all about it, today, with this little G-string on.
nanda. tībakku haitenjan, omae sōtō yaru ki manman janē kā yo.
なんだ、ティーバックはいてんじゃん、お前相当や
る気満々じゃねーかーよ

These are my "strictly business" panties. I shaved down there.
shōbu shitagi nanōo. paipan shichatta no.
勝負下着なのーー。パイパンしちゃったの

You're all smooth.
nanka tsuru tsuru
なんかつるつる

Lick my clit! Ah! Right there!
kuri chan nametēe. a! soko soko!
栗ちゃんなめてーー。あ！そこそこ！

Your cunt is drenched.
omae no manman, mō chō gucho gucho dayo.
お前のマンマン、もう超ぐちょぐちょだよ

Your cock. It's so hard. I want to suck it for you.
ochin chin. nanka sugoku. bin bin shiteru. watashi ga namete ageru.
おチンチン、なんかすごく、ビンビンしてる。私が
舐めてあげる

I'm gonna stick my hot rod so deep into you.
motto oku made ore no atsui no wo irete ageru yō.
もっと奥まで俺の熱いのを入れてあげるよー

God, I can't take it anymore! Put it in!!! P—please!
mō damē gaman dekinaīi. naka ni irete. ho...hoshī
もうだめぇ我慢できないーー。中に入れて。ほ…ほ
しい。

Fuck. I'm about to come already.
yabai. ore, mō ikisō.
やばい。俺、もう逝きそう。

What? Seriously? Premature ejaculation?
e? maji de? moshiya sōrō?
え？まじで？もしや早漏？

I'm ... I'm going to come! Where do you want it?
ore mō dechau yo. doko ni hoshī?
おれ。もう出ちゃうよ。どこに欲しい？

I want to drink it.
gokkun shitai no.
ごっくんしたいの。

I'm gonna rope all over your face.
gasha shite yarū.
顔射してやるう。

Ah, it's so hot. Yummmm!
ā atsui. oishī.
あー熱い。おいしい。

Man, I love that dirty sex.
maji konna hentai purei tte chō kimochi ī.
マジこんな変態プレイって超気持いいーー。

premature ejaculation
sōrō
早漏

impotent
impo
インポ

horny bastard
etchi
エッチ

sadist
sado
サド

masochist
mazo
マゾ

pervert
sukebe
スケベ

foot fetishist
ashi-fetchi
足フェッチ

CHAPTER 6

ANGRY JAPANESE

MUKA MUKA NIHONGO

むかむか日本語

•••••Enemies

teki

敵

The old axiom holds true in any country: for every good soul there are two assholes driving slow in the passing lane. So I guess it makes sense that there are twice as many ways to describe personality flaws as there are to compliment somebody.

Boss

buchō

部長

My **boss** is a total fucking asshole.
uchi no **buchō** wa maji mukatsuku
うちの**部長**はマジむかつく。

Ex-boyfriend
motokare
元カレ

My **ex-boyfriend** was seriously evil.
atashi no **motokare** wa hontō ni
saiaku na yatsu datta
あたしの元カレは本当に最悪
なヤツだった。

Ex-girlfriend
motokano
元カノ

My **ex-girlfriend** was a slutty bitch.
ore no **motokano** wa shō mo nē yariman datta
俺の元カノはしょーもねーヤリマンだった。

Stalker
sutōkā
ストーカー

Seriously, I've got like three **stalkers** right now, and it's
driving me nuts.
maji de **sutōkā** ga sannin mo ite sa komatteru no yo
マジで**ストーカー**が三人もいてさ、困ってるの
よ。

Sex predator
chikan
痴漢

A **sex predator** tried to feel me up on the subway.
chikatetsu de **chikan** ni atte, atai no mune o sawarō to
shiteita no
地下鉄で痴漢に遭って、あたいの胸をさわろう
としていたの。

Cheapskate
kechi
ケチ

My old man is a **stingy** bastard.
uchi no oyaji wa dai no **kechi** da
うちの親父は大のケチだ。

Lazy bitch
guzu
グズ

My old lady is a **lazy** bitch who sits around watching daytime TV.
ofukuro wa **guzu** de sa waidoshō bakkari miteyagaru
おふくろはグズでさ、ワイドショーばっかり見てやがる。

Mother-in-law
giri no okāsan
義理のお母さん

My **mother-in-law** is the devil.
giri no okāsan wa onibaba da
義理のお母さんは鬼婆だ。

Lawyer
bengoshi
弁護士

Lawyers kind of suck, don't they?
bengoshi tte amari ī inshō nai yo ne
弁護士ってあまりいい印象ないよね？

Politician
seijika
政治家

I wonder if Japanese **politicians** are as dirty as American ones?
nihon no **seijika** wa amerika no seijika hodo kitanai no kashira
日本の政治家はアメリカの政治家ほど汚いのかしら？

Cops
satsu
サツ

The **cops** keep picking on me because I'm a foreigner.
gaijin dakara **satsu** ni ayashimarete bakkari da
外人だから**サツ**に怪しまれてばっかりだ。

┈┈ Smacktalk
waruguchi
悪口

Oh my god, did you *hear* her Japanese slang? She sounded like a total tourist bitch! She must spend so much time on that skanky hairdo that she doesn't have time to study up on her Japanese smacktalk. The polite little slut.

He/she is such a **liar**.
aitsu wa **usotsuki** da
あいつは**嘘つき**だ。

He/she totally **thinks he's the shit**.
aitsu wa **chōshi ni notteiru** yo ne
あいつは**調子にのっている**よね。

He/she must think he/she is too **cool** for school.
aitsu wa jibun no koto o mecha **kakkō ī** to omottendaro
あいつは自分のことをめちゃ**格好いい**と思ってんだろ。

He/she is such an **asshole**.
aitsu wa **kanji warui** kara
あいつは**感じわるい**から。

Oh my god, he/she is so **creepy**.
aitsu wa hontō ni **kimoi**ndakara
あいつは本当に**キモイ**んだから。

He/she has been **talking shit** about me.
aitsu wa ore no **warukuchi** o itteiru
あいつは俺の**悪口**を言っている。

He/she always **stands me up at the last minute.**
aitsu wa itsumo **dotakyan** suru
あいつはいつも**ドタキャン**する。

He/she is so **self-centered.**
aitsu wa chō **jikochū** da
あいつは超**自己中**だ。

He/she is **no fun** at all.
aitsu wa **tsumannai** yatsu da
あいつは**つまんない**ヤツだ。

All she ever does is **hang out** with her boyfriend.
anoko kareshi to **asonde** bakka damon
あの子、彼氏と**遊んで**ばっかだもん。

He/she is totally a **Benedict Arnold.**
aitsu wa **uragirimono** da
あいつは**裏切り者**だ。

We used to be friends, but **not anymore.**
mukashi wa tsurundeta kedo **ima wa sappari** da ne
昔はつるんでたけど、**今はさっぱり**だね。

He/she **pisses me off.**
aitsu wa **atama ni kurun** da
あいつは**頭に来るん**だ。

Oh my god, **I cannot stand** him/her!
maji **mukatsuku** aitsu
マジ**むかつく**、あいつ！

He/she really **gets on my nerves.**
aitsu maji **uzē**
あいつ、マジ**うぜー**。

We'll never **make up.**
nakanaori wa mō muri da na
仲直りはもう無理だな。

I never want to see them again.
mō nido to **aitakunai**
もう二度と**会いたくない**。

⋯⋯ Getting pissed off

mukatsuku

むかつく

When something pisses you off, it's really important to be able to express that anger, because otherwise your eyes will roll back into your head and you'll never be able to see again.

He/she...
aitsu...
あいつ…

His/her attitude...
aitsu no taido...
あいつの態度…

His/her face...
aitsu no kao...
あいつの顔…

The way he/she talks...
aitsu no shaberikata...
あいつのしゃべり方…

Everything...
nani mo kamo...
何もかも…

You...
omae...
おまえ…

Fat Americans...
debu na amejin...
デブなアメ人…

...piss(es) me off.
...mukatsuku
…むかつく。

...really piss(es) me off!
...maji mukatsukū
…マジむかつくー！

* The word 「マジむかつく」 (maji mukatsukū) sometimes gets abbreviated as "MM," as in the following:

...bother(s) the hell out of me.
. . .ni hara ga tatsu
…に腹がたつ。

...get(s) my tits in a wringer.
. . .wa atama ni kuru wa
…は頭に来るわ。

...get(s) on my nerves.
. . .ki ni kuwane
…気にくわねー。

Oh my god, his/her face **pisses me off so much.**
chikushō aitsu no kao chō emu emu da
ちくしょー、あいつの顔、超MMだ。

·····Snapping
kireru
キレる

If Step One of anger is getting pissed off, then Step Two is snapping. The Japanese word for snapping, *kireru*, means exactly the same thing: the delicate thread suspending your overwrought composure has just snapped in half with an unbecoming twang.

He/she called me fat and I **snapped.**
aitsu ni debu tte iwarete **kireta**
あいつにデブって言われて**キレた**。

He/she **looses their shit** really easily.
aitsu wa sugu **kireru** mon
あいつはすぐ**キレる**もん。

Don't snap at me!
kireru na yo
キレるなよ！

Another word you will hear in this context is *gyaku gire* (逆ギレ), which literally means "snapping back"—like when you yell "Fuck you" out the window at a Chinese lady who just cut you off, only to have her blue-haired head come poking out of her Oldsmobile to yell "YEAH, WELL FUCK YOU TOO, MOTHERFUCKER" in a voice that leaves the next four generations of your children in shame.

I tried snapping at my girlfriend, but she just **snapped back harder.**
kanojo ni kirete mitara **gyakugire** sarechatta
彼女にキレてみたら**逆ギレ**されちゃった。

He/she gave me a **dirty look.**
aitsu ni **gantsuke** rareta
あいつに**ガンつけ**られた。

You always **look pissed off** in photographs.
omae shashin de wa itsumo **gantsukuteteiru**nda yo na
おまえ、写真ではいつも**ガンつけてる**んだよな。

I just wanna **haul off and deck** that motherfucker.
bunnagutte yaritē
ぶん殴ってやりてぇー。

⋯⋯Fighting
kenka
けんか

Ever since World War Two, Japan has been a peaceful country in which the word "fighting" has no meaning. Just kidding! Even though guns are illegal in Japan, a fair amount of shit gets kicked, some of it even memorably violent. My dirty mouth has gotten me black eyes and a busted jaw, plus one time I saw a couple tweakers totally brain a kid with a *mountain bike*. Oh yeah, and I got a knife pulled on me once in Shinjuku, but that was by a creepy Russian dude. Still, the language barrier often prevents foreigners from getting involved in some of the best bloodletting that the Eight Islands have to offer—so get yourself some good health insurance and try out the following:

You suck.
saitei da omae
最低だお前。

Fuck off.
uzēndayo
うぜーんだよ。

Motherfucker.
kisama
貴様。

Asshole.
temē
てめぇー。

Leave me the fuck alone.
shitsukēndayo
しつけーんだよ。

I hate you.
daikirai
大嫌い。

What did you just say!?!
nandatō
なんだと…！？！

Get out of my way.
doke
どけ。

Go to hell.
shine
死ね。

Eat shit.
kusokurae
くそくらえ。

Shut the fuck up.
ussēndayo
うっせーんだよ。

What the fuck?
ahoka
アホか？！

You're worthless.
tsukaenē yatsu dana
つかえねーやつだな。

You got a problem?
monku akka
文句あっか？

Bring it on!
kakatte koi
かかってこい！

·····Stopping a fight
kenka o tomeru
けんかを止める

If you ever have one of those rare holiday experiences when a carload of teenage meth-heads roll up on you fully intending to make your jaw a permanent part of the curb, you might have one of those transcendental moments where you realize that Phish isn't such a horrible band and that John Kerry wasn't necessary a total pussy for leaving Vietnam to protest war—and before you know it you are saying one or more of the following in an Owen Wilson drawl:

Don't get your panties all in a knot.
atama o hiyashitoke
頭を冷やしとけ。

Hey, **calm** the fuck **down.**
oi **ochitsuke** yo
おい、**落ち着け**よ。

Dude, don't **loose your shit** like that.
sonna ni **kireru** na yo
そんなに**キレる**なよ。

Take a **deep breath** or something.
shinkokyū demo shiro
深呼吸でもしろ。

You're all **worked up.**
kōfun shisugi dayo
興奮しすぎだよ。

Violence is bad.
bōryoku wa ikenai zo
暴力は行けないぞ。

Give **peace** a chance, man.
heiwa ga ichiban sa
平和が一番さ。

I'm a **pacifist**.
watashi heiwa shugisha nandesu
私、平和主義者なんです。

Forget **about it**, man.
hottoke yo
ほっとけよ。

I have **nothing to do** with this.
kotchi kankei nē yo
こっち関係ねーよ。

Who really **gives a fuck**?
dōdemo injanē ka
どうでもいいんじゃねーか。

Stop it.
yamero
やめろ。

Whatever, man.
katte ni shiro
勝手にしろ。

Call the **cops**.
keisatsu o yobe
警察を呼べ。

·····Pigs
satsu
サツ

"Pig," an old-timers' and high-school wiggers' word for "cop," certainly doesn't apply to all officers of the law. I use the word "pig" here (and the corresponding *satsu*, which doesn't describe actual swine) strictly to refer to *Japanese* cops, who belong to that special category of douchebag that is all douche and no bag. I mean, Japanese cops must have absurdly tiny dicks, because every one of them walks around like they've got something huge to prove. Maybe it's because they didn't get to go to college and have uninhibited sex, or maybe it's just because they aren't allowed to carry guns. Japanese cops are also totally racist, so watch out if you look the least bit foreign. If you happen to be black or Chinese, you might as well just start running the other way.

The **pigs** are coming.
satsu ga kuru zo
サツが来るぞ。

Run away!
nigero
逃げろ！

Oh, shit.
yabē
やべー。

It's a biker cop!
shirobai da
白バイだ！

Hide **the shit.**
yaku o kakuse
ヤクを隠せ。

Act like **you don't know shit.**
shiranpuri shiro
知らんぷりしろ。

I don't know **anything.**
nani mo shiranainda
何も知らないんだ。

Fucking **cops.**
porikō no aho
ポリ公のアホ。

CHAPTER 7

POPPY JAPANESE

POPPU NA NIHONGO

ポップな日本語

▪▪▪▪▪ Music

ongaku

音楽

Speaking objectively, I have to warn you that Japanese pop music is relentlessly horrendous crap. This is a quantified fact, but it's also one of the world's great mysteries. I mean, Japanese visual arts are uniformly amazing, right? Japanese fashion is light years ahead of everybody. Japanese cuisine is nothing less than delectable. And Japanese video games have invented the industry. So why is J-Pop so unlistenable? Oh yeah …They don't have black people in Japan.

Let's listen to some…

. . .kikō ze

…聴こうぜ。

Do you listen to...
...wa yoku kiku
…はよく聴く？

Do you know where can I hear some...
... o kikeru toko wakaru
…を聴けるトコわかる？

J-Pop
jē poppu
Jポップ

At least it's not reggaeton.

Johnny's Music
janīzu kei
ジャニーズ系

The Japanese version of "boy bands." Arashi, Smap,
V6, Kinki Kids—these NAMBLA posterchildren make the
Backstreet Boys look like they actually have testicles.

Indies
indīzu
インディーズ

Has little in common with "indie rock." Basically, it's J-Pop
that doesn't have big-label backing. Mostly awful.

Reggae
regē
レゲェ

Even Japanese kids are rocking the dreads these days.
Like white reggae, but even more misguided.

Hip-hop
hippu hoppu
ヒップホップ

Japan has produced some quality DJs—just don't give
them a mic, and everything will be cool.

Jazz
jazu

ジャズ

Japanese people have great taste in jazz—check out the Tokyo Blue Note.

Soul
sōru

ソウル

Thank you, Japanese record labels, for reprinting all of my favorite albums. I really appreciate it, but will you stop charging me 3,000 yen a pop?

Rock-n-roll
rokku

ロック

The one genre that even Japan can't fuck up. X Japan forever.

Techno
tekuno

テクノ

Something tells me that Japan would be pretty good at this, but I don't know because I don't listen to poo.

What bands do you like?
sukina **bando** wa

好きなバンドは？

Who's your favorite singer?
sukina **kashu** wa

好きな歌手は？

Show me a cool Japanese band.
nihon no omoshiroi bando o **shōkai shite**

日本の面白いバンドを紹介して。

Do you play any instruments?
nanika **gakki** wa dekiru

何か楽器はできる？

The chorus is really catchy.
sabi no tokoro ga omoroi
サビのところが面白い。

I'm really into moshing.
suramu dansu ga daisuki
スラムダンスが大好き。

·····Comedy
owarai
お笑い

The best thing about Japanese TV is the comedy shows. Japanese comedians will do just about anything for a laugh, and you don't have to deal with crappy sketch comedy or stand-up. Being able to understand the jokes is reason enough to learn the language, but it's also a huge part of the culture. Everyone from kids to adults knows the major comedy groups and their shows, and can riff on their favorite punchlines.

ᴄ ESSENTIAL COMEDY WORDS:

What the fuck?
nande yanen
なんでやねん！

This is the classic response to a joke. If someone makes a bad pun, or pokes fun at you, just look outraged and say "*Nande yanen!*"

Tsukkomi
突っ込み
tsukkomi

A *tsukkomi* is a joke at someone's expense. You notice something funny about someone, and make a *tsukkomi* about it.

Are you retarded?
ahoka
アホか！

A very general *tsukkomi*.

Retard
boke
ボケ

This is the one the *tsukkomi* is directed at. All the great Japanese comedians usually come in pairs: one *tsukkomi* and one *boke*.

Punch line
ochi
オチ

Don't always expect jokes to have them.

Pun
gyagu
ギャグ

Japanese people have a humorous love/hate relationship with them.

Horrendous pun
oyaji gyagu
親父ギャグ

The kind that will get your ass thrown in the punitentiary.

Quit it with the shitty puns.
oyaji gyagu iunatchū nen
親父ギャグ言うなっちゅーねん。

This story has no punch line!
ochi ga naijan kono hanashi
オチがないじゃん、この話！

Stop making fun of me!
sonna ni tsukkomu na
そんなに突っ込むな！

What are you talking about, retard?
nani ittendayo boke
何言ってんだよ、ボケ！

•••••The Major Comedy Acts
omona owarai konbi
主なお笑いコンビ

...are hilarious.
. . .wa waraeru yone
…は笑えるよね。

Downtown
dauntaun
ダウンタウン

Downtown is the best, not just because they have been around forever but because they are just malicious enough to make you laugh and wince at the same time.

London Boots
ronbū
ロンブー

London Boots hails from Tokyo, and they like to play pranks on unsuspecting people. A lot of it involves catching people who cheat on their boyfriends/girlfriends and publicly humiliating them.

Ninety Nine
nainai
９９（ナイナイ）

Ninety Nine is a lot like Downtown—a duo from Osaka that moved to Tokyo and diversified. Okamura is funny and looks like a chimpanzee, but Downtown is still cooler.

Neptune
nepuchūn
ネプチューン

Neptune is a 3-man comedy group, not as raunchy or edgy as some others, although they used to work with a comedian named Becky who is like a prettier, funnier version of Christina Ricci. Becky, will you go to the prom with me?

Akashiya Sanma
sanma san
さんまさん

Akashiya Sanma is the O.G. Japanese comedian. He's like Johnny Carson. His buckteeth are an icon of the entire Japanese entertainment industry.

••••• Comics and cartoons
manga to anime
漫画とアニメ

Man, some American kids are really into *manga* and *anime*! I don't get what they like about it so much, or why they choose the *anime* that they do, but are they ever crazy about it. One thing is for sure, though: these kids are enjoying it in an entirely different way than their Japanese counterparts. I'm hoping that the following phrases may help open up a dialogue between the nerd communities of our two great countries so we can solve this mystery once and for all.

moē
萌え…

A word expressing a nerd's deep affection for an animated character, or some trait thereof (i.e., the most important word a nerd can know).

I'm so **in love** with this character's kitty-cat ears!
kono kyara no nekomimi ni **moē**
このキャラの猫耳に**萌え**…！

I'm mad about that maid outfit!
ano meidofuku ni **moemoe**
あのメイド服に**萌え萌え**！

What character do you **get all MOE** about?
ichiban **moeru** kyara tte dāre
一番**萌える**キャラってだ…れ？

⊂ NYYYYERRRRDS
otaku
オタク

I'm proud of being a **nerd!**
jibun wa **otaku** de aru koto o hokori ni omotte imasu
自分は**オタク**であることを誇りに思っています。

We're both **nerds.**
uchira wa **otaku dōshi** dane
うちらは**オタク同士**だね。

That person is **kind of nerdy.**
ano hito wa **otakkī na kanji**
あの人は**オタッキーな感じ**。

Do you think Japanese is a **nerdy** nationality?
nihonjin wa **otakkī** na kokumin da to omou
日本人は**オタッキー**な国民だと思う？

I'm a total … nerd.
jibun wa … **otaku** desu
自分は…**オタク**です。

I'm really into…
…ni hamatte imasu
…にハマっています。

computer
pasokon
パソコン

anime
anime
アニメ

comic book
manga
漫画

professional wrestling
puroresu
プロレス

‹ CARTOONS
anime
アニメ

Robot anime
robotto anime
ロボットアニメ

These are the staple of Japanese cartoons: Gundam, Mazinger, Macross, Transformers.

Transformation anime
henshin anime
変身アニメ

This implies a cartoon where pretty girls transform into superheroes in skimpy clothing: Sailor Moon, Cutie Honey, Pretty Cure, etc.

Studio Ghibli
jiburi anime
ジブリアニメ

Studio Ghibli produces some cartoons that are so good they aren't even nerdy. *Spirited Away* and *Totoro* were big hits overseas, and *Nausicaa* is still the greatest animated feature ever.

⊂ COMICS
manga
漫画

Tachiyomi
立ち読み

Tachiyomi is the practice of standing in a bookstore or convenience store reading the books without ever buying any. A brilliant way to kill time.

I stood reading ...for a whole hour!
o ichijikan mo tachiyomi shiteta
…を一時間も立ち読みしてた。

Jampu
ジャンプ

Jampu is the classic comic periodical, home to such greats as *Kinniku Man, Dragon Ball, Slam Dunk,* and *One Piece.*

Magajin
マガジン

Magajin has published *Tensai Bakabon, Kyojin no Hoshi, Goddohando Teru,* and *Hajime no Ippo.*

Nakayoshi
なかよし

Nakayoshi is a comic periodical for girls, home of *Sailor Moon, Kyandī Kyandī,* and *Ojamajo Doremi.*

Ribon
りぼん

Ribon is the main competitor to Nakayoshi, publishing *Chibi Marukochan, GALS!,* and *Mimi o Sumaseba.*

Dōjinshi
同人誌

Dōjinshi are privately published comic books, a lot of which feature homosexual characters.

Komike
コミケ

Komike is the annual comic market, a huge event where people come to sell their *dōjinshi*.

‹ HERO SHOWS
ヒーロー番組

Power Rangers
gorenjā
5 レンジャー

The Power Rangers was a remix of this classic Japanese hero show. Spandex, karate, and plotlines bordering on abstractions.

Masked Rider
kamen raidā
仮面ライダー

The Masked Rider is a guy who transforms into a gigantic superhero on a motorcycle with special grasshopper powers.

Ultraman
urutoraman
ウルトラマン

Ultraman is the granddaddy of all hero shows. He shoots a "Specium Beam" out of his hand and can fly with jet-propelled boots.

‹ OTHER ANIME / MANGA RELATED ACTIVITIES

Cosplay
kosupurei
コスプレ

"Cosplay" is the practice of dressing up like your favorite animated characters. It's like yiffy but not quite as creepy.

Maid cafes
meido kissa
メイド喫茶

This is a café where guys go to be served by girls dressed up in maid outfits, like the girls in a comic book.

Butler cafes
shitsuji kissa
執事喫茶

Girls, as well, can go have their coffee served by men in butler outfits. It's only fair.

Action figures
figyua
フィギュア

Action figures are very popular among the *otaku* crowd. You don't play with them—you just set them on the top of your bookshelf and sigh, "*Moē...*"

Plastic models
puramo
プラモ

Plastic models may be the kind of thing that your dad played with, but in Japan they are still very popular.

Goth/Lolita fashion
gosurori kei
ゴスロリ系

Goth/Lolita fashion is basically just goth for little Japanese girls. Cute and scary, like everything else in Japan.

⊂ FAMOUS QUOTATIONS FROM ANIME AND MANGA:

"Settle down, settle down. Take a breather, take a breather." (Ikkyū-san)
awatenai awatenai. hitoyasumi hitoyasumi. (Ikkyū-san)
あわてないあわてない。ひとやすみひとやすみ。（一休さん）

"A pig that can't fly is just a plain old pig." (Crimson Pig)
tobenē buta wa tada no buta da. (kurenai no buta)
飛べねぇ豚はただのブタだ。（紅の豚）

"I chastise you, in lieu of the moon!" (Sailor Moon)
tsuki ni kawatte oshioki yo! (sērā mūn)
月に代わってお仕置きよ！（セーラームーン）

"Hola, ami-gonad." (Obotchama-kun)
tomodachinko! (obotchama kun)
ともだちんこ！（おぼっちゃまくん）

"Good enough for me." (Tensai Bakabon)
korede, ī no da. (tensai bakabon)
これで、いいのだ。（天才バカボン）

⋯⋯Fashion
fasshon
ファッション

If you take anything home with you from Japan, don't let it be some crappy oriental bric-a-brac like paper lanterns or teacups. Don't try to subtly show off your worldliness to your friends with crappy lacquered chopsticks. Take home clothes, man. Tokyo is full of rare vintage garments, shoes you won't find in America for another decade and denim that makes Diesel look like Faded Glory.

⊂ I WANT TO DRESS...

no fukusō ga shitai

…の服装がしたい。

Visual
bijuaru kei

ビジュアル系（V系）

"Visual" fashion is based on eighties hair-band fashion. You may notice that a lot of Japanese rock bands still dress like eighties hair-bands—this is where "Visual" fashion comes from.

Abercrombie
abakuro kei

アバクロ系

"Abercrombie" fashion is just what you'd think. In Japan, an Abercrombie shirt is kind of secret code that you're gay.

Mod
mōdo kei

モード系

"Mod" fashion is pretty much the same everywhere.

Vintage
furugi

古着

"Vintage" fashion is an integral part of the Japanese wardrobe.

B
bīkei

B系

"B" stands for "black," as in "That Japanese dude in the Fubu shoes must think he's black."

Gyaru
gyaru kei
ギャル系

"Gyaru" fashion is a uniquely Japanese phenomenon. Shocking blond hair, heavy fake tans, white eye makeup, fluorescent colors and miniskirts of breathtaking scantiness.

Conservative
konsaba kei
コンサバ系

"Conservative" fashion stresses basic elegance, avoiding gaudy or trendy clothes. Young businesswomen in Tokyo have this down—clean-cut but sexy.

Young Lady
onē kei
お姉系

"Young Lady" fashion stems from "Gyaru" fashion. The blond hair, tans, and miniskirts are still there, to some extent, but the color schemes have mellowed into earth tones, and the accessories are brand name. Think of it as "Gyaru" meets "Conservative."

Military
miritarī kei
ミリタリー系

"Military" fashion may sound like an oxymoron, but camo jackets and green/gray color schemes make for some stylish outfits.

Gothic
goshikku kei
ゴシック系

"Gothic" fashion in Japan is just what you think it is, without the Columbine threat of violence.

Gothic Lolita
gosurori kei
ゴスロリ系

"Gothic Lolita" fashion is creepiness plus cuteness. Like a Tim Burton movie!

‹ THAT OUTFIT LOOKS REALLY...
sono fukusō wa… dane
その服装は…だね。

stylish
oshare
おしゃれ

cute
kawaī
かわいい

lame
dasai
ださい

slutty
eroi
エロい

hideous
yabai
ヤバい

‹ HE/SHE IS SO…
ano hito wa … dane
あの人は…だね。

hyper-tanned
ganguro
ガン黒

fair-skinned
bihaku
美白

cool
kakko ī
カッコイイ

handsome dude
ikemen
イケメン

pretty girl
bijin
美人

popular with the opposite sex
mote mote
モテモテ

like a model
moderu mitai
モデルみたい

nerdy
otakkī
オタッキー

CHAPTER 8

SPORTY JAPANESE

SUPŌTĪ NA NIHONGO

スポーティーな日本語

●●●●●Sports
スポーツ

supōtsu

Fuck love—sports is the real universal language. Catholics, Muslims, Jews, and Buddhists will never love each other, but they all certainly enjoy a good game of *futtobōru*. In Japan, the most popular dialects of this universal language are baseball, soccer, kickboxing, golf, and sumo. Most other sports are also played and appreciated somewhere—even women's ice hockey!

Do you play…
. . . yatteiru
…やっている？

I want to play…
. . . yaritai
…やりたい。

Let's watch the ... game.
. . .no shiai miyō ze
…の試合見ようぜ。

soccer
sakkā
サッカー

baseball
yakyū
野球

kickboxing
kē wan
K 1

golf
gorufu
ゴルフ

basketball
basuke
バスケ

rugby
ragubī
ラグビー

tennis
tenisu
テニス

American football
amefuto
アメフト

sumo
sumō
相撲

If you're in Japan, be sure to take the opportunity to watch a sumo match. It's incredible live, but even on TV it never fails to entertain.

Explain the rules of sumo to me.
sumō no rūru o setsumei shite kudasai
相撲のルールを説明してください。

Americans would be great sumo wrestlers, they're all so fat.
amejin wa minna debu de sumō ni muiteiru kamo
アメ人はみんなデブで相撲に向いているかも。

What... do you like?
sukina ... wa
好きな…は？

sports
supōtsu
スポーツ

teams
chīmu
チーム

players
senshu
選手

·····Minor sports
mainā supōtsu
マイナースポーツ

Around the major entertainment hubs of Tokyo (Shinjuku, Shibuya, Ikebukuro, and so on), you'll find places to play all the world's minor sports—ping-pong, bowling, pool, darts, air hockey, batting cages, and spin-the-bottle. If you ever miss the last train, try hitting up the minor-sports circuit to polish the old token-insertion skills.

Wanna go play some...
yari ni ikō ka
…やりに行こうか？

ping-pong
takkyū
卓球

bowling
bōringu
ボーリング

pool
biriyādo
ビリヤード

darts
dātsu
ダーツ

air hockey
eāhokkē
エアーホッケー

batting cages
battingu
バッティング

mahjong
mājan
麻雀

•••••Cheering
ōen
応援

This may disappoint all the aspiring hooligans out there, but Japanese sports fans are oppressively polite. They don't get drunk, jeer the opposing team, or yell slogans about the refs' mothers (with the exception, perhaps, of Hanshin baseball fans). Oftentimes there are special team songs that you can learn, but for the most part you can just stick to the following simple cheers:

Go!
gambarē!
がんばれーーー！

Fight!
faito
ファイト！

Hurray!
furē furē
フレーフレー！

Put 'em away
shimattekō
しまってこー！

Banzai!
banzai
万歳！

Where is the cheering section?
ōendan wa doko ni irundesu ka
応援団はどこにいるんですか？

Will you teach me the team cheer?
ōenkyoku oshiete kuremasu ka
応援曲教えてくれますか？

The ref is a retard!
shimpan no boke
審判のボケ！

Swwwing, batterbatterbatter!
battā ga senpūki da
バッターが扇風機だ！

* This literally means "the batter is an electric fan"—he flails around and hits nothing but air.

Where can I find a scalper?
dafuya o sagashite irundakedo
ダフ屋を探しているんだけど。

For which team are you a...
dochira no...
どちらの…

supporter
sapōtā
サポーター

fan
fan
ファン

hooligan
fūrigan
フーリガン

·····Exercise
undō
運動

There are plenty of places to work out in Tokyo, from fitness clubs to rock-climbing gyms. But if you want to be like a real Japanese person, you'll go down to the river and hit some golf balls at the old ladies walking their dogs.

Where's a good place to do some...
...dekiru toko wakaru
…できるトコわかる？

exercise
undō
運動

weight training
kintore
筋トレ

jogging
jogingu
ジョギング

yoga
yoga
ヨガ

swimming
suiei
水泳

stretching
sutoretchi
ストレッチ

situps
fukkin undō
腹筋運動

pushups
udetate fuse
腕立て伏せ

pullups
kensui
懸垂

sprints
supurinto
スプリント

treadmill
toreddomiru
トレッドミル

practice
renshū
練習

I want to work out my...
... o kitaetainda
…を鍛えたいんだ。

abs
fukkin
腹筋

biceps
nitō kin
二頭筋

triceps
santō kin
三頭筋

pecs
kyōkin
胸筋

thighs
futomomo
太もも

calves
fukurahagi
ふくらはぎ

cremaster
seisō kyokin
精巣挙筋

Let's go for a **run.**
jogingu ikō ze
ジョギング行こうぜ。

Want to go to the **gym?**
fittonesu sentā ikō ka
フィットネスセンター行こうか？

Would you **spot** me?
chotto **hojo** shite moraemasu ka
ちょっと補助してもらえますか？

I've started to **sweat.**
ase kaichatta
汗かいちゃった。

I'm exhausted.
tsukaretā
疲れたー。

I'm **out of breath.**
ikigire shichatta
息切れしちゃった。

I'm all sore today.
kyō wa kin'nikutsū da
今日は筋肉痛だ。

·····Video games
gēmu
ゲーム

Video games are to Japan what tea is to Britain or war is to
America. Visiting the pristine temples of Kyoto won't teach you
a third of what you will learn about Japan at the video arcade.

Do you have...
... motteru
…持ってる？

Wanna play some...
... yarō ka
…やろうか？

Are you good at...
... umai no
…うまいの？

Playstation
puresute
プレステ

Nintendo Wii
uī
ウィー

X-box
ekkusu bokkusu
Xボックス

The original NES
famikon
ファミコン

Dance Dance Revolution
danrebo
ダンレボ（DDR）

The kids get pretty serious about this one.

The crane machine
yūfō kyatchā
UFOキャッチャー

The one where you grab toys with the crane claw.

Dragon Quest
dorakue
ドラクエ

The best-selling Japanese game ever. Final Fantasy is a derivation of this.

Animal Crossing
oideyo dōbutsu no mori
おいでよ、どうぶつの森

A really popular game for Nintendo DS.

Mario Cart
mario kāto
マリオカート

A world standard.

Let's go to the arcade.
gēsen ikō ze
ゲーセン行こうぜ。

I'm not a **gamer** or anything, but I like video games.
gēmā to made ikanai kedo kekkō suki da yo
ゲーマーとまでいかないけど、結構好きだよ。

CHAPTER 9

HUNGRY JAPANESE

PEKO PEKO NIHONGO

ペコペコ日本語

••••Belly
hara
はら

Food is pretty popular everywhere, but it holds a particularly important place in the hearts of the Japanese. You can't hold a conversation for more than thirty seconds without someone recommending a restaurant or sharing a recipe with you, which is kind of counterintuitive considering how skinny most Japanese folks are. Every day is Iron Chef to these people—a fact which is quite pleasing to the belly but which taxes your vocabulary when it comes time to articulate your appetites.

⊂ MY BELLY IS...
onaka ...
おなか…

growling
goro goro itte yagaru
ゴロゴロ言ってやがる

famished
hettanā
へったなー

starving
peko peko damon
ペコペコだもん

full
ippai
いっぱい

stuffed
pampan
パンパン

hurting
itai
痛い

·····Food
meshi
メシ

Technically, *meshi* is the word for rice. But of course, everybody knows that all Asian people ever eat is rice! So in Asia the word "rice" just means "food." Kind of like how in America the word "Jack in the Box" means breakfast, lunch, and dinner.

...food
meshi ...
メシ…

Did you already eat...?
... kutta
…食った？

I want to EAT…!!!
… kuitē
…食いてぇーーー！

I love….
… daisukī
…大好きぃ…。

What kind of… do you feel like?
wa dōshiyō
…はどうしよう？…

What's your favorite…?
ichiban sukina … wa
一番好きな…は？

Why don't I fix you some…?
… tsukutte ageyō ka
…作ってあげようか？

I want some cheap, greasy…!
yasukute aburappoi … ga kuitai
安くて油っぽい…が食いたい！

Wanna order some takeout…?
… wa demae tanomō ka
…は出前頼もうか？

·····Excuse me!

sumimasen
すみません

Tipping is not practiced in Japan. But it's completely acceptable to get the waiter's attention by banging on your table and throwing silverware while yelling "sumimasen!" Waiters are basically at your beck and call. On the other hand, it's not acceptable practice to ask for certain ingredients to be left out of a dish, or for less salt, or for a doggy bag to take your leftovers home in. The following sorts of situations are where you want to use *sumimasen*.

⊂ EXCUSE ME, BUT...

sumimasen...

すみません …

. . .can we order?
...chūmon shite mo ī desuka
…注文してもいいですか？

. . .what do you recommend?
...nanika osusume wa arimasu ka
…何かお薦めはありますか？

. . .how much is this?
...kore ikura desu ka
…これ、いくらですか？

. . .will this make me full?
...kore de onaka ippai ni nareru kana
…これでおなかいっぱいになれるかな？

. . .what's in this?
...kore wa nani ga haitteirundesu ka
…これは何が入っているんですか？

. . .can I get one of these?
...kore o kudasai
…これをください。

. . .can I get a menu?
...me'nyū o kudasai
…メニューをください。

. . .this tastes weird.
...kore aji ga hen desu ga
…これ、味が変ですが。

. . .does this have MSG?
...aji no moto wa haitte masu ka
…味の素は入ってますか？

. . .can I get some water?
...mizu o kudasai
…水をください。

. . .can I get a fork?
. . .fōku o kudasai
…フォークをください。

. . .what's the holdup?
. . .zutto matte irundesu ga
…ずっと待っているんですが。

. . .can I have your phone number?
. . .denwabangō o oshiete kuremasen ka
…電話番号を教えてもらえますか？

·····Yummmmm!

umē
うめー！

Did you know that the way a person eats is a direct reflection of how they make love? Some people are speed-eaters, others are notoriously picky. Some people like greasy shit, and others like it bland. Lots of dudes are into the Asian food, these days. Personally, the girls I date like to eat four meals a day. Oh yeah, and vegetarians like to have sex with plants, which makes Japanese TV pure porn, because it's chocked full of food programming. The roots of soy sauce, the secret to delicious beef curry, the best *ramen* shops in Osaka—food culture has found its medium in Japanese television. And on these innumerable food programs, every time the hosts put something new in their mouths they inevitably make some comment about how delicious it is, so as to convey to their viewers at home the complex gustatory sensations occurring in their mouths. The meaning of these comments basically boils down to "DELICIOUS!!!!" but they take on a number of forms, including the following:

This is **good.**
kore **oishī** ne
これ、おいしいね。

This is **delicious!**
koitsu wa **umai** wa
こいつはうまいわ！

Fantabulous!
geki uma
激ウマ！

It **melts** in my mouth.
kuchi no naka de **torokete kurū**
口の中でとろけてくるぅ…。

It smells **fucking fabulous.**
sungē ī kaori
すんげーいい香り。

Holy shit, this is **scrumptious.**
uwa kore **maji umē**
わ、これ、マジうめぇー。

Can I get **seconds?**
okawari moraemasu ka
おかわりもらえますか？

I want to **marry** the cook.
tsukutta hito to **kekkon** shitai
作った人と結婚したい。

You **mao'd that shit down.**
omae **paku paku kutta** nā
お前、ぱくぱく食ったなー。

You **scarfed** it on down.
mogu mogu kutteta mon
もぐもぐ食ってたもん。

·····Food benders
kuidaore
食い倒れ

A "food bender" (*kuidaore*) is a Japanese tradition wherein you spend an entire evening walking from restaurant to restaurant, progressively gorging yourself into glassy-eyed stupor. This practice originated in the Osaka area, but it's just as easy to eat yourself silly on gourmet cuisine in any of Tokyo's 23 wards.

⊂ LET'S GET SOME...
...ni shiyō
…にしよう。

Japanese food
washoku
和食

beef rice bowl
gyūdon
牛丼

This is Japanese fast food: cheap and filling. You can find college kids horfing this shit down in any of the ubiquitous chain restaurants purveying these beef feasts: Yoshinoya, Matsuya, Kōbe Ranputei.

egg noodles
rāmen
ラーメン

Not the shitty instant noodles that got you through college. Real Japanese *ramen* is the stuff of dreams. There are whole magazines devoted to finding the best *ramen* in Tokyo.

Korean barbecue
yaki niku
焼き肉

This has little to do with the soul food you are probably accustomed to. Thin slabs of top-grade beef, often marinated, that you grill at your table.

Japanese pancake
okonomi yaki
お好み焼き

Based on a cake of batter and cabbage, okonomiyaki is kind of like pizza in that it allows you to add pretty much whatever you feel like: bacon, seafood, veggies, cheese, noodles, kimchee.

chicken kabobs
yakitori
焼き鳥

Yakitori is usually sold by street vendors, and comes in a wide variety of forms: chicken breast, chicken wings, chicken cartilage, chicken liver, chicken skin.

breaded pork
tonkatsu
とんかつ

Basically this is a deep-fried pork cutlet.

Japanese stew
oden
おでん

You know it's winter, in Japan, when the convenience stores pull out these big vats of broth and start stewing stuff: eggs, potatoes, *daikon*, tofu, *kamaboko*. Trust me on this: the stuff at 7-Eleven is actually really good.

soups
nabemono
鍋物

Nabemono is an umbrella term for a number of soup dishes, including *sukiyaki* and *shabushabu*.

tempura
tempura
天ぷら

This is like the assorted deep-fry platter you get at an Applebee's or some shit like that.

Chinese food
chūka
中華

Japanese Chinese food is like a less greasy version of American Chinese food, with higher quality ingredients, prettier waitresses, and no Spicy Wings.

curry
karē
カレー

You can get Indian-style curry in Japan (check out Jimbōcho in Tokyo), although the word *karē* implies Japanese curry, which is more sweet than spicy.

French food
furansu ryōri
フランス料理

A lot of Japanese cooks actually go to France to study foreign cooking, so French food in Japan is probably more authentic than what you get in America, although I wouldn't know because I never eat the shit.

Italian food
itaria ryōri
イタリア料理

Don't expect to find a lot of heavier dishes like lasagna in Japan, but if you're into spaghetti and other noodle dishes, Japanese spaghetti is pretty damn good. They generally serve pretty shitty wine, though.

▪▪▪▪▪ Fast food
fāsuto fūdo
ファーストフード

Of course you can find a McDonald's in even the most remote corner of the Eight Islands, and a hamburger there tastes pretty much the same as the one you ate in whatever Middle American town you may have come from. But if you're going to eat fast food in Japan, I suggest you try one of the following native franchises, in descending order. Americans have a lot to learn about their own cuisine.

‹ LET'S GO TO...
... ikō ze
…行こうぜ。

Mos Burger
mosu
モス

Mosu is like the In-N-Out of Japanese fast food. They use quality beef and have all sorts of weird experimental burgers.

First Kitchen
fakkin
ファッキン

Pronounced like "fucking," these places are cheap, quick, and popular among high school kids.

Freshness Burger
furesshunesu bāgā
フレッシュネスバーガー

Freshness Burger is kind of a health-conscious burger joint. Unfortunately, that makes it less tasty than a Mos Burger, although it's light years ahead of McDonald's.

Lotteria
rotteria
ロッテリア

The name "Lotteria" makes it sound like they should be selling scratch-offs instead of burgers and fries. It's like McDonald's but not made out of poo.

Kentucky Fried Chicken
kenta
ケンタ

Except for very remote parts of Hokkaido, it is impossible to find turkey in Japan, so it has become tradition to get Kentucky Fried Chicken for Christmas dinner—and eat only the skin.

McDonald's
makku
マック

The Golden Arches. The only exciting thing about Japanese McDonald's is that you can get corn soup there.

●●●●●Family restaurants
famiresu
ファミレス

Have you ever been to a Denny's where they have a drink bar? You pay like three bucks to drink all the coffee and orange juice and soda you want. Drink bars are pretty standard at Japanese family restaurants, as well—but the exciting thing is that some places—like Bāmiyan and Birudi—will occasionally have hard drink bars, too, where you pay a nominal fee for all the wine and liquor your composure can handle.

⊂ LET'S GO TO...

... ikō ze
…行こうぜ。

Royal Host
roiho (roiyaru hosuto)
ロイホ（ロイヤルホスト）

Royal Host is the standard-bearer for all family restaurants. A lot of meat-based dishes on the menu.

Denny's
denīzu
デニーズ

Denny's in Japan is so much nicer than Denny's in America. Clean and tasty, with Japanese and American food.

Gusto
gasuto
ガスト

Gusto is cheap and easy. It's popular with college and high school kids.

Jonathan's
jona (jonasan)
ジョナ（ジョナサン）

Jonathan's is kind of cheap and dirty. You see a lot of angry parents and whiny kids there.

Casa
kāsa
カーサ

Casa has a lot of Salisbury steaks, curry, and omelet dishes. None of which are great.

Saizeriya
saize (saizeriya)
サイゼ（サイゼリヤ）

Saizeriya is an Italian family restaurant—like Olive Garden except edible.

Bāmiyan
bami (bāmiya)
バミ（バーミヤン）

Bāmiyan is a Chinese family restaurant. The food isn't great and the service sucks, but the one by my house had the **hard drink bar.**

Yumean
yumean
夢庵

The Chinese food at Yumean isn't that great, either, but I would place it an inch or so above Bāmiyan.

Don
don (sutēki no don)
どん（ステーキのどん）

"Don," as this steak house is affectionately called, makes a damn good steak. Applebees, Chili's, Outback—they don't got shit on the Don.

Bikkuri Donkey
donkī (bikkuri donkī)
ドンキー（びっくりドンキー）

Bikkuri Donkey does not purvey donkey-based cuisine. They specialize in Salisbury steaks, and do a good job with it.

Bldy
birudi
ビルディ

Bldy (this is the actual spelling) has a very eclectic menu, but none of it is great. Fortunately, they are reputed to have the **hard drink bar.**

·····Cafés
kissaten
喫茶店

Starbucks is every bit as ubiquitous in Tokyo as in New York and has better coffee than other chain alternatives. But if you're a hippie who feels like Starbucks harshes your socially conscious mellow, check out some of the Japanese coffeehouses. Doutor has bagel sandwiches!

Starbucks
sutaba
スタバ

Like Japanese bra sizes, drinks at a Japanese Starbucks are all one size smaller than their name suggests, so that a "medium" corresponds to a "small" in America.

Doutor
dotōru
ドトール

At Doutor, you get these exhausted businessmen chain-smoking and drinking coffee next to bag ladies mumbling into their teacups. The coffee ain't great, but the atmosphere has no pretensions.

Segafredo
segafurēdo
セガフレード

Segafredo specializes in sticky drinks like the "Pina Colada Yogurt Granita." They are leading the whole Frappuccino genre into the 21st century.

Renoir
runoāru
ルノアール

Pretentious and froufrou, Renoir is the type of place that frowns on to-go orders and prefers for you to sit down with all the other widowed madams until you order a tiramisu out of sheer anxiety.

·····Sushi expert
sushi tsū
寿司通

Oh, you thought Japanese slang was just for punkass kids? Well, tell that to the septuagenarian chef behind the sushi bar pulling his knife through a yellowtail with all the precision of a brain surgeon. He still has shrapnel in his knee from the Russo-Japanese war and knows more sushi slang than a rapper knows Ebonics. So try out some of these words next time you're at a sushi restaurant and see if nobody notices that you're a big fat American who rubs his chopsticks together and then orders a Coke with his California roll.

‹ CAN I GET SOME...
. . .kudasai
…ください。

water
ohiya
おひや

soy sauce
murasaki
ムラサキ

tea
agari
あがり

ginger
gari
ガリ

check
oaiso
おあいそ

Can I get it sans wasabi?
sabinuki de onegai shimasu
サビ抜 きでお願いします。

What kind of sushi do you like?
sukina osushi wa
好きなお寿司は？

You don't eat California rolls so much in Japan, eh?
kariforunia rōru wa nihon ja amari kuwanai ne
カリフォルニアロールは日本じゃあまり食わな
いね。

·····Yuck!
mazui
まずい！

In my experience, it's pretty hard to find food in Japan that
is actually *bad*. Even the hot lunches served at the poorest
elementary school in Japan are light years tastier than the shit
that Americans eat. If you're British, even homeless people in
Japan eat better than you. But let's imagine that you *do* get
served something that doesn't taste quite right while you're
in Japan. Be sure to express your discontent immediately
and vocally, because by now you probably already have
food poisoning.

This tastes **weird.**
aji ga chotto **hen** da
味がちょっと変だ。

This **tastes bad.**
mazui na kore
まずいな、これ。

Seriously, this is **fucking gross.**
iya gekimazu da nā
いや、激マズだなー。

This is total **shit.**
kuso dayo kore
クソだよ、これ。

This is a **shit among shit.**
kuso no naka no kuso dane
糞中の糞だね。

Seriously, we are eating **poo.**
unko da ne maji de
うんこだねマジで。

I can't fucking eat this.
konna mono **kuenē**
こんなもの食えねー。

This restaurant **fucking sucks.**
kono mise wa saitei saiaku
この店は最低最悪。

Is this Korea? Because this shit **tastes like** *dog.*
koko wa kankoku? datte **inu no aji ga suru**nda mon
ここは韓国？だって犬の味がするんだもん。

This shit would taste better after I **puked it back up** and ate it.
kore o **hakimodoshite** mō ikkai kutta hō ga zettai oishī shi
これを吐き戻してもう一回食った方が絶対おいしいし。

We got better meals than this **in prison.**
gokuchū no meshi no hō ga yoppodo umakatta shi
獄中のメシの方がよっぽどウマかったし。

Let's go.
ikō yo
行こうよ。

Wanna pull an **eat-and-run?**
kuinige shiyō ka
食い逃げしようか？

·····Picky Eaters

kuwazu girai

食わず嫌い

Kuwazu-girai is a game that Japanese folks like to play at *izakaya* and other restaurants that have small, tapas-like dishes. The premise of the game is this: everybody orders three things—two they absolutely love and one they can't stand. Japanese *izakaya* usually have extensive enough menus so that it's easy to find something you hate. Then you take turns consuming your three dishes under the scrutinizing gazes of your companions, and they try to guess which was the one that you actually hate. Most people don't realize what bad actors they are, and nothing is funnier than watching a bad actor act—especially when they are overcompensating for nausea by pretending to savor and relish something that is making them sick. It's a great way to get to know people's culinary and dramatic inclinations—and a rare opportunity to eat fermented soy beans. *Bon appétit!*

·····Other Ulysses Press Titles

Dirty Italian: Everyday Slang from "What's Up?" to "F*%# Off!"
GABRIELLE EUVINO, **$10.00**

Nobody speaks in strictly formal address anymore. Certainly not in Italy, where the common expression shouted on the streets is far from textbook Italian. This all-new, totally-up-to-date book fills in the gap between how people really talk in Italy and what Italian language students are taught.

Daidōji Yūzan's Code of the Samurai: A Contemporary Dual-Language Edition of the 16th-Century Bushido Shoshishu
A. L. SADLER, **$10.95**

Presents the classic teachings that guided samurai behavior and formed the foundation for which Japanese society is based. This easy-to-read version stays true to the original teachings while offering guidance and wisdom that remain as timely as ever.

The Art of War
SUN TZU, TRANSLATED BY LIONEL GILES, **$12.95**

This Ulysses Press edition directly parallels but greatly improves on a poor-quality self-published version that has proven popular by offering the same classic Lionel Giles translation and the same dual language Chinese/English layout.

Skater Girl: A Girl's Guide to Skateboarding
PATTY SEGOVIA & REBECCA HELLER, **$14.95**

Reveals the ins and outs of skateboarding to young women who know that sporting some road rash is one off-the-hook lifestyle statement.

Total Heart Rate Training: Customize and Maximize Your Workout Using a Heart Rate Monitor
JOE FRIEL, $14.95

Shows anyone participating in aerobic sports, from novice to expert, how to increase the effectiveness of his or her workout by utilizing a heart rate monitor.

Complete Krav Maga: The Ultimate Guide to Over 230 Self-Defense and Combative Techniques
DARREN LEVINE & JOHN WHITMAN, $21.95

Developed for the Israel military forces, Krav Maga has gained an international reputation as an easy-to-learn yet highly effective art of self-defense. Clearly written and extensively illustrated, *Complete Krav Maga* details every aspect of the system including hand-to-hand combat moves and weapons defense techniques.

To order these books call 800-377-2542 or 510-601-8301, fax 510-601-8307, e-mail ulysses@ulyssespress.com, or write to Ulysses Press, P.O. Box 3440, Berkeley, CA 94703. All retail orders are shipped free of charge. California residents must include sales tax. Allow two to three weeks for delivery.

●●●●●About the Author

Matt Fargo is the owner of one of the world's dirtiest mouths. He has worked in Japan as a writer, translator, and musician among other things, subsequently earning his Master's degree in Japanese Literature at UC Berkeley. He currently lives in New York, where he enjoys the metropolitan propensity for filthy language. If you get good enough at Japanese, you can read his first book, 「空想英語読本」, or you can check out his other projects at matthewfargo.com.

GET D!RTY

Next time you're in Japan or just chattin' in Japanese with your friends, drop the textbook formality and bust out with expressions they never teach you in school, including:

- ◆ **cool slang**
- ◆ **funny insults**
- ◆ **explicit sex terms**
- ◆ **raw swear words**

Dirty Japanese teaches the casual expressions heard every day on the streets of Japan:

What's up?	Ossu?
How's it hanging?	Chōshi dōyo?
I'm smashed.	Beron beron ni nattekita.
I love ginormous tits.	Kyo'nyū daisuki.
Wanna try a threesome?	Yatte miyō ka sanpī?
I gotta take a leak.	Shonben shitē.
He's such an asshole.	Aitsu wa kanji warui kara.

$10.00 U.S.

Distributed by
Publishers Group West

Ulysses
Press